THE TEJAS STORY

The Light Combat Aircraft Project

THE TEJAS STORY

The Light Combat Aircraft Project

AIR MARSHAL PHILIP RAJKUMAR (RETD)

MANOHAR
2026

First published 2008
Reprinted 2026

ISBN 978-81-7304-764-0

Published by
Ajay Kumar Jain *for*
Manohar Publishers & Distributors
4753/23 Ansari Road, Daryaganj
New Delhi 110 002

Typeset by
Kohli Print
Delhi 110 051

Printed and bound in India

I dedicate this book to
my wife Sheila
who followed an airman's flight
and always made a home

Contents

List of Illustrations 9

Preface 11

Abbreviations 15

1. First Flight 19
2. The Long Road to First Flight 27
3. Change of Guard 34
4. Early Life and My Career in the IAF 42
5. The Aeronautical Development Agency 62
6. Quadruplex Digital Fly-by-Wire and the Glass Cockpit 70
7. In Flight Simulation and Roll Out of TD-1 80
8. Engine Ground Run, Pokharan Blasts, US Sanctions and RTS Problems 95
9. The Iron Bird and Taxi Tests 105
10. The Patna Air Crash and Preparations for First Flight 119
11. Honours and Awards, Aero India 2001 and Completion of the First Block of Flights 131
12. Delay in the First Flight of TD-2 and Negotiations with Foreign Companies 140
13. Flutter, the Naming Ceremony, Supersonic Flight and Retirement 154
14. Postscript 162

Index 167

Illustrations

PLATE *between pages 88–9*

1. The author on commissioning, 10 November 1962
2. LCA TD-1 getting airborne on its first flight on 4 January 2001 at Bangalore
3. Wg. Cdr. Rajiv Kothiyal climbing out of the cockpit of the LCA TD-1 after the historic first flight on 4 January 2001
4. The author being congratulated by the Defence Minister, Shri George Fernandes, after the first flight of TD-1 Seen in the background is ACM A.Y. Tipnis and at the edge of the picture is Dr. V.K. Aatre DG, ADA
5. Group photograph in front of TD-1 after first flight
6. Wg. Cdr. Rajiv Kothiyal receiving the Iven Kinchloe trophy from Iven Kinchloe Jr., at the SETP Awards ceremony at the Beverley Hilton Hotel, Los Angeles, USA on 27 September 2001
7. 3-View drawing of LCA TD-1
8. Three Axes of an aircraft
9. First Flight of TD-2 on 6 June 2002
10. NFTC personnel in early 1995
11. CLAW evaluation on the T-33A at the Niagara Falls Air Force Base in the USA in June 1995
12. CLAW evaluation on the F-16 VISTA at Buffalo, NY, USA in July 1996
13. T-33 and F-16 VISTA in formation in July 1995
14. Group photograph with Dr V.K. Aatre at Aero India, 2003
15. Formation take off of LCA TD-1 and TD-2 in the presence of Prime Minister A.B. Vajpayee on 4 May 2003
16. The author being greeted by the Defence Minister, Shri George Fernandes, after the naming ceremony on 4 May 2003
17. Group photograph with the Prime Minister Atal Behari Vajpayee after the naming ceremony on 4 May 2003

18. Presenting a photograph of two Tejas aircrafts flying in formation to President Abdul Kalam at Rashtrapati Bhavan on 25 August 2003
19. No. 1 Squadron pilots at Adampur after the September 1965 Indo-Pak war
20. MIG-23 evaluation in the Soviet Union in April 1979
21. The author when he was Chief Test Pilot at ASTE in 1986
22. The author being greeted by Air Cmde. A.K. Nagalia, Commandant ASTE after his 3261st flight on the MIG-21 on 8 August 2001, his 60th birthday
23. Visit to the General Electric jet engine plant at Lynn, Massachusetts, USA in July 2002
24. Tejas being demonstrated at Aero India 2005
25. Tejas seen in IAF grey colour scheme with drop tanks, bombs and CCM
26. PV-2 takes off on its first flight on 1 December 2005
27. PV-2 on its first flight on 1 December 2005
28. MMR test bed AVRO in flight September 1997
29. The author with Sheila (left) and Nilima (centre) in December 1998
30. The author on retirement from the IAF on 31 August 2001

Preface

I have written this book about the nine years that I spent working in the technology demonstration phase of the LCA programme. I have relied mainly on my memory and on my working diaries of those years. The book starts with an account of the first flight of the LCA Technology Demonstrator aircraft on 4 January 2001. Chapters 2 and 3 give background information related to the genesis of the project while Chapter 4 gives a brief account of my life from the time I was born till I came to ADA. Chapters 5 through 13 are about my stay at ADA. The book is written as a first person narrative, because it deals with events viewed from my perspective as the person in charge of the flight test programme. There is always a danger of placing excessive emphasis on one's role in events in which one has played a part, but in any aircraft development programme, flight testing and finding solutions for design deficiencies uncovered in the process is a crucial phase. Problems identified must be solved as they never go away and failure to do so usually spells the death of a project.

Once the aircraft started flying there was the ever-present possibility of a mishap and flight safety became the most important priority of the flight test team. At the same time risky tests had to be performed and these had to be planned with care. The first flight of a prototype is one such case and the several new technologies packed into the LCA, especially the digital fly-by-wire flight control system increased the risk severalfold. It must be remembered that the technology transfer sanctions imposed by the USA after the Pokharan nuclear tests in May 1998 were in place for 31 months preceding first flight, and continued till completion of the first block of 12 flights.

A large number of men and women from many organizations

contributed to the success of the technology demonstration phase. I refer to them in the book as Team LCA.

Apart from the numerous technical challenges Team LCA had to overcome, the biggest challenge was managing people. Personnel from different organizations and work cultures had to come together and work in harmony. As in all such situations personality clashes occurred, and took up quite a bit of the time and effort of the top managers to solve. I had my fair share of such problems in the flight test team. I have described events exactly as they occurred and quoted personalities verbatim. The intention was to present a factually accurate record of events and not to defame any person or organization.

My narrative follows a chronological sequence from the time I arrived on deputation at the Aeronautical Development Agency in 1994 till I finally retired from Government service in 2003. I have included my involvement in two major aircraft accident inquiries, and my dialogue with Air Headquarters to get my rightful promotion as these were activities in which I had to invest time and effort during that period.

The reader must know that commercial contracts with six well-known Western companies helped speed up the project considerably. Dassault Aviation of France was involved in the Project Definition Phase (PDA). Lockheed Martin, USA provided crucial assistance for development of the digital fly-by-wire flight control system. Calspan, USA, Wright Laboratories of the USAF and British Aerospace (now BAE Systems) UK provided invaluable support to our control engineers who developed the control law for the flight controls. BAE Systems also provided support for building the first set of composite wings, integration of the flight control system in the airframe and helped in preparations for flight testing the aircraft. GE (Engines Division) USA supplied the engine and provided integration and maintenance support. Alenia of Italy manufactured the first five sets of composite skins for the wings till our own autoclave became ready. It will be no exaggeration to say that the technology demonstration phase would not have succeeded without the participation of these companies.

Chapter 14 is a postscript which deals with the relevance of the Tejas in the IAF inventory and the gains of the LCA project. Lastly, in order to avoid too frequent use of the first person in my narrative I have used 'we' not in the royal sense but to mean Team LCA.

Bangalore
October 2007

AIR MARSHAL P. RAJKUMAR
(RETD)

Abbreviations

ACAS	Assistant Chief of the Air Staff
ACM	Air Chief Marshal
ADA	Aeronautical Development Agency
Ada/FORTRAN	Software Languages
ADE	Aeronautical Development Establishment
AGL	Above Ground Level
ALH	Advanced Light Helicopter
AM	Air Marshal
AMAGB	Aircraft Mounted Auxiliary Gear Box
AMLCD	Active Matrix Liquid Crystal Display
AMSL	Above Mean Sea Level
AOC-in-C	Air Officer Commanding-in-Chief
AR&DC	Aircraft Research and Design Centre of HAL
ASIEO	Advanced Systems Integration and Evaluation Organization
ASR	Air Staff Requirement
AST	Air Staff Target
ASTE	Aircraft and Systems Testing Establishment
ATC	Air Traffic Control
AVSM	Ati Vishisht Seva Medal
AVM	Air Vice Marshal
BAe	British Aerospace now BAE Systems
BVR	Beyond Visual Range
CAD	Computer Aided Design
CAM	Computer Aided Manufacture
CAS	Chief of the Air Staff
CCM	Close Combat Missile
CDR	Crash Data Recorder
CEF	Cockpit Evaluation Facility
CEMILAC	Centre for Military Airworthiness & Certification

CFD	Computational Fluid Dynamics
CG	Centre of Gravity
CLAW	Control Law
CRE	Chief Resident Engineer
CSIO	Central Scientific Instruments Organization
CTP	Chief Test Pilot
CVRDE	Combat Vehicles Research and Development Establishment
DAIR	Dynamic Avionics Integration Rig
DASR	Director Air Staff Requirements
DBU	Digital Back Up
DERA	Defence Evaluation and Research Agency
DFCC	Digital Flight Control Computer
DGAQA	Directorate General of Aeronautical Quality Assurance
DGCA	Directorate General of Civil Aviation
DRDO	Defence Research and Development Organization
ECS	Environmental Control System
EGR	Engine Ground Run
ELS	Engineer in Loop Simulator
EMC	Electro Magnetic Compatibility
EMI	Electro Magnetic Interference
EPNER	Ecole du Personnel Navigant d'Essais et de Reception, the French Test Pilots School
FADEC	Full Authority Digital Engine Control
FCN	Flight Clearance Note
FCOC	Fuel Cooled Oil Cooler
FCS	Flight Control System
FMCD	Flight Mechanics and Controls Division of NAL
FOC	Final Operational Clearance
FRD	Functionality Requirement Document
FRRB	Flight Readiness Review Board
FTE	Flight Test Engineer
FTIE	Flight Test Instrumentation Engineer
FTP	Flight Test Panel

GE	General Electric
GOI	Government of India
GPS	Global Positioning System
GTRE	Gas Turbine Research Establishment
HAL	Hindustan Aeronautics Limited
HUD	Head Up Display
HQ	Handling Qualities
IAF	Indian Air Force
IFS	In Flight Simulation
IJT	Intermediate Jet Trainer
INS	Inertial Navigation System
IOC	Initial Operational Clearance
ISRO	Indian Space Research Organization
IV&V	Independent Verification and Validation
JFS	Jet Fuel Starter
Kmph	Kilometres per hour
KRA	Key Result Areas
KVA	Kilo Volt Amperes
LAH	Light Attack Helicopter
LCA	Light Combat Aircraft
LM	Lockheed Martin
LRUs	Line Replaceable Units
MFD	Multi Function Display
MMR	Multi Mode Radar
MMCS	Martin Marietta Control Systems
MOD	Ministry of Defence
MOU	Memorandum of Understanding
Mph	Miles per hour
NAL	National Aerospace Laboratories
NATO	North Atlantic Treaty Organization
NFTC	National Flight Test Centre
OFP	Operational Flight Programme
PEC	Pressure Error Correction
PBIT	Pilot Built In Test
PCT	Programme Co-ordination Team
PD(TD)	Project Director (Technology Development)
PDP	Project Definition Phase

PIL	Pilot in Loop
PLOC	Probability of Loss of Control
PMO	Prime Minister's Office
PV	Prototype Vehicle
PVC	Performance Verification Committee
PVSM	Param Vishisht Seva Medal
RFA	Request for Action
RM	Raksha Mantri (Defence Minister)
RTS	Real Time Simulator
SA to RM	Scientific Adviser to Raksha Mantri
SCT	Structural Coupling Test
SETP	Society of Experimental Test Pilots, USA
SPS	Secondary Power System
TD	Technology Demonstrator
USAF	United States Air Force
VCAS	Vice Chief of the Air Staff
VIP	Very Important Person
VISTA	Variable Inflight Simulation Training Aircraft

CHAPTER 1

First Flight

4 January 2001. I woke up at 5:30 a.m. with a feeling which was a strange mixture of anticipation, confidence and a vague fear of the unknown. A lot was at stake for Indian aeronautics that day. It was the day the Light Combat Aircraft (LCA), Technology Demonstrator-1 (TD-1) was to take to the air for the first time, and I, as the man in charge of the flight test programme, was responsible for the safety of the test flight. The telephone rang at 6:30 a.m. It was Dr Kota Harinarayana, the Programme Director, confirming that the aircraft had completed its pre-flight checks and was being towed to the flight line. Though the planned take-off was at 10 a.m., the flight briefing was to start at 8 a.m. I raced to the National Flight Test Centre (NFTC) located at the HAL airport, Bangalore.

Shortly after I got there, Dr V.K. Aatre, Scientific Adviser to the Raksha Mantri and Director-General, Aeronautical Development Agency, Dr Kota, and Mr K. Nagraj, Chief Executive of the Centre for Military Airworthiness and Certification arrived. I had requested the Chief of the Air Staff (CAS), Air Chief Marshal Anil Tipnis, to be at NFTC by 7:45 a.m. for the briefing as he was going to pilot one of the two Mirage 2000 chase aircraft. He arrived five minutes early, and after a quick pre-flight medical conducted by Sqn. Ldr. Anjali Alam of the Institute of Aerospace Medicine, for the five pilots involved in the day's flying, we assembled in the briefing room.

42 year-old Wg. Cdr. Rajiv Kothiyal (Kothi), a graduate of the United States Air Force Test Pilots School, was the pilot chosen for the hazardous mission. Hazardous, not because of

negligence on any one's part, but because of the many new technologies in the aircraft, especially the quadruplex digital fly-by-wire Flight Control System (FCS) and the 'glass' cockpit, both of which had been developed indigenously for the first time.

The briefing began and Kothi did not show any sign of nervousness. In fact, he exuded an air of quiet confidence as he described the flight profile and told the crew of the two chase aircraft, what exactly he expected of them in the event of an in-flight emergency. We ran through an elaborate list of emergencies that could occur and discussed the action to be taken for each eventuality. Two helicopter crews were also present; one was to be on airborne standby with a doctor on board and one on the ground. The weather was fine with cloudless skies and light winds. Ideal conditions for the first flight of a prototype.

I went with Kothi to the flight line where the aircraft was parked. It was all white as prototype aircraft are usually painted in a high visibility paint scheme for ease of optical tracking. It looked beautiful and had IAF roundels on its wings and the tricolour flash on the tail fin. The tail number was KH 2001 in honour of Dr Kota Harinarayana and the year of the first flight.

Though no official announcement of the first flight had been made, HAL and ADA personnel had thronged vantage points on the roofs of surrounding buildings not wanting to miss watching Indian aviation history being made. Kothi finished his walk around inspection of the aircraft and I said 'Kothi, we have done our homework well. The flight controls and all systems have behaved perfectly during the ground tests and high speed taxi runs. You shouldn't have a problem. Best of luck.' Of course my heart was in my mouth as I spoke but I did not let my feelings show. Dr Kota also came and wished Kothiyal the very best. A number of VIPs who were not present at the briefing had gone straight to the viewing point by the side of the runway.

I rushed back to the telemetry monitoring control room

and positioned myself next to Wg. Cdr. Raveendran (Ravi), the test director who was in front of the master monitoring console. Ravi was a Flight Test Engineer who had graduated from the Ecole du Personnel Navigant d'Essais et de Reception (EPNER) France and had spent six years in the LCA programme. He had profound knowledge of every system on the aircraft. The prototype was extensively instrumented with 400 parameters being acquired from critical systems and telemetered in real time to the ground station. A further 800 parameters were being acquired and stored in a tape recorder on board. We had 16 monitoring consoles in the room, each console manned by a systems specialist keeping a watchful eye on the performance of his or her system. The engine, fuel, hydraulics, electrics, environmental control, brakes, flight control system, vibrations and strains at critical locations on the airframe were being monitored for the flight. Video cameras located with the telemetry antenna gave the test director a good view of the aircraft on the flight line as well as the runway in use and the approach funnel. None of the other specialists could see the video screen and all the curtains were drawn to permit them to concentrate on monitoring the performance of their system, and to report immediately any anomaly noticed to the test director on the intercom.

Air Marshal J.S. Rai, the Air Officer Commanding-in-Chief, Training Command, IAF walked into the room and sat down next to me. I ordered the door to be closed and looked at my watch. It was 9:15 a.m. The radio crackled to life and Kothi's voice came over the air asking Ravi to start the pre-flight checks. Shortly thereafter he started the GE F 404 engine and all the monitoring consoles came alive with system indications. The two Mirage 2000 chase aircraft, the primary chase aircraft piloted by Wg. Cdr. Raghunathan Nambiar (Nambi), also started up. The after-start checks, radio checks with the chase aircraft and the Air Traffic Control (ATC) tower went through without a hitch, but took 30 minutes. Only the final hurdle remained.

All aircraft fitted with fly-by-wire flight control systems have to perform an automatic Pilot (initiated) Built In Test (PBIT) of the system after engine start. This required a button to be pressed by the pilot after which the flight control computer took over and ran through a pre-programmed sequence of tests at the end of which a green GO lamp flashed in the cockpit. In an aircraft in service it took about a minute. In a prototype it was more elaborate and took 10–12 minutes. When Kothi initiated the test, I kept my fingers crossed as we had had test failures in the past. A first time failure of the PBIT to pass would call for a repeat of the test. A second-time failure would require the test flight to be aborted for the day. The airfield had been closed only for an hour from 10 a.m. to 11 a.m. and it was already 9:47 a.m. The minutes went by with agonizing slowness and after what seemed an eternity, to my great elation I saw the green GO lamp shining on the aircraft's main instrument console. Kothi asked for taxi instructions from the ATC tower. It was exactly 10 a.m.

On the video screen I saw the two Mirages move out of the parking area and enter the taxi track. The LCA followed them. The east-facing Runway 09 was in use and Kothi headed for the line up point. It was a glorious sight to behold! Blue skies, bright sunshine and the LCA in gleaming white, majestically rolling down the taxi track with thousands of people watching from the rooftops of every building in sight. As the aircraft neared the runway the brake specialist called out a failure in one of the two control lanes available in the brake by wire system. Ravi looked at me for a decision and I flashed him a thumbs up sign as I was aware of the redundancies available to bring the aircraft to a stop on the landing roll. After a final check of the aircraft by the wheels and tyres check team, Kothiyal took permission and entered the live runway.

The two Mirages were airborne by this time, but Kothi could roll only when Nambi gave him a radio call to do so, indicating that he was correctly positioned to quickly join up with the prototype after it got airborne.

Kothi opened full power on the engine and did a final check of the flight controls. All 16 specialists confirmed to Ravi that all systems were 'GO' and Ravi cleared Kothi to roll. Nambi's call came and Kothi released brakes. I saw the aircraft accelerate rapidly down the runway. Kothi called 'Rotating' and raised the nose wheel. Seconds later the LCA lifted off gracefully. It was 10:18 a.m. The next few seconds would tell us whether the years of toil Team LCA had put in developing the FCS would come to naught or not. Kothi's call 'And climbing' set those fears at rest as we now knew the FCS was working as it should.

I was just about to begin breathing normally when the telemetry auto tracking system failed and all 16 screens started showing erroneous readings. There was no way of knowing what was happening in the innards of the aircraft! Ravi asked, 'Shall I call him back?' Chase aircraft are provided to enable the test team to cope with such eventualities. I said 'Tell Nambi to move into close formation and check the aircraft for fuel and hydraulic leaks or other signs of abnormal behaviour'. Kothi said that his cockpit readings were fine and the aircraft was flying normally. Nambi reported no sign of any abnormality. I decided to continue with the planned flight profile and told Ravi to inform the pilot of my decision. Kothi agreed with me and continued with the flight. I aged a lot in those few seconds!

The flight profile called for a climb to 3 km (10000 ft), a slow down to approach speed, a practice circuit at that height, some gentle turns and a return to base. The wheels were left in the down and locked position throughout as aircraft wheels are the only known objects in the physical world which do not obey Newton's law of gravitation! Sometimes they go up and don't come down and we did not want that kind of excitement on the first flight!!

Kothi flew the planned profile and said the aircraft was behaving more or less in the same way as it did in the simulator on which he had practised the profile over and over again for the past few weeks. Soon it was time to land and Kothi positioned himself on a 10 km long straight-in approach to Runway 09. When he was about three minutes away on approach, the telemetry antenna locked on to the aircraft and data reappeared on the screens. Ravi asked the systems specialists to confirm that all was normal, and to my great relief and everyone else's they reported all systems were GO.

We saw the LCA with the two Mirages escorting it appear on the video screen. It was a sight which will remain etched in my memory for the rest of my life. Everyone tensed up as the crucial first landing was about to take place. Kothi's voice remained calm when he asked ATC for landing instructions. He flew a steady approach, flared the aircraft over the runway and executed a flawless touch down on the main wheels. He lowered the nose wheel on to the runway and deployed the tail chute. The Mirages came down low and did a go around. As the aircraft slowed down to taxiing speed, he jettisoned the chute and turned off the live runway. The time was 10:36 a.m. The first flight had lasted only 18 minutes but heralded a renaissance of Indian aeronautics that will enable this country to assume its rightful place amongst the aeronautical powers of the world in the years to come.

As Kothi parked the aircraft and switched off the engine, there were wild scenes of jubilation amongst the HAL and ADA personnel. Someone even held the Tricolour aloft symbolizing a moment of national pride. When Kothi came down the ladder he was mobbed by the workers and carried on their shoulders for some distance. A huge gathering of VIPs thrust their way forward, each one intent on marking his presence in the photographs which were being shot by the hundreds. After considerable effort I was able to go up to Kothi and shake his hand!

At the debriefing session the room was crowded with the who's who of Indian aeronautics. Kothi was congratulated by the Raksha Mantri George Fernandes and the CAS. We looked at the video camera footage shot from the chase aircraft and the data captured on the telemetry screens during the all important take-off and landing phases of flight. Every system on board the aircraft had worked perfectly. It is a mandatory requirement in test flying to list out all anomalies noticed, from engine start to shut down to enable the designers and technicians to take remedial action and clear the aircraft for the next test flight. When Kothi filled in the snag sheet he wrote 'Nil snags'. There could have been no more fitting tribute to the professionalism, industry and dedication of Team LCA and it was my privilege to have been part of that team.

After the debriefing was over, Dr Kota told me that ADA personnel were waiting for Kothi and me to go to ADA. When we drove to the ADA entrance gate, a huge crowd of ADA personnel, both men and women were waiting for us with garlands. As we got out of the car, crackers went off and both Kothi and I were carried on the shoulders of excited men all the way from the gate to the porch which was a distance of about 75 yards. It was an unforgettable experience!

Later that day I ordered an investigation into the telemetry problem. It turned out that a software technology park in Bangalore had been using the precise frequency on which the LCA telemetry signal was being transmitted. The telemetry auto track antenna had locked on to the signal, as it was stronger than that of the LCA. We were blissfully unaware of this misuse of our frequency!

After Kothi had flown the first six flights I sent in his nomination for the prestigious Iven Kinchloe Award to the Society of Experimental Test Pilots (SETP) in the USA. The SETP gives this award every year for the most significant achievement in experimental test flying during the year under consideration. Very few in India seemed to have realized the significance of the achievement of safely flying a prototype with so many new technologies on board. However, the SETP awards committee which consisted of a group of very experienced test pilots who had seen many programmes worldwide thought differently and had no hesitation in giving the Iven Kinchloe Award for the year 2001 to Rajiv Kothiyal. I was very happy that Team LCA's monumental effort had been recognized by a bunch of hard-nosed professionals.

No Indian test pilot has ever received this award in the past. Without exaggeration, the Iven Kinchloe Award can be called the 'Oscar' for experimental test flying. In the finest traditions of the IAF, Wg. Cdr. Rajiv Kothiyal had truly touched the skies with glory.

CHAPTER 2

The Long Road to First Flight

The military precision with which the events of the day of the first flight unfolded and the flawless performance of the prototype, gave many people the erroneous impression that what had been achieved was easy and inconsequential. The Raksha Mantri, George Fernandes, told us much later that on the day preceding the first flight, a foreign aerospace company had written to him warning him of catastrophic consequences, if he permitted the first flight to take place. Their view was that the FCS software had not been developed with adequate rigour and had not been validated properly. It is therefore very important for me to set the record straight and give the reader an insight into the challenges overcome by Team LCA, while developing the aircraft.

The LCA story actually began in the late 1970s. Air Chief Marshal I.H. Latif was the CAS from 1978 to 1981. He was unhappy with the in-service performance of the HAL upgraded Gnat, the Ajeet fighter. The aircraft had severe limitations of payload, range and serviceability and did not fit into the planned re-equipment of the IAF fighter fleet. He was also aware of the need to phase out some of the earlier versions of the Mig-21 in the mid-1990s. He therefore asked HAL to design a relatively low-cost replacement for the Ajeet and the Mig-21.

In 1980 India was able to successfully put a 40 kg satellite into low earth orbit and join a very select club of nations with that capability. The Indian Space Research Organization (ISRO) and its engineers received well-deserved kudos in the national and international media. Unfortunately, the aeronautical community had nothing remotely as significant as the

Rohini to show for their existence since the 1940s. When some leading aeronautical personalities approached Prime Minister Indira Gandhi in the early 1980s with a request to be given a chance to prove their design capabilities, she took the bold step of asking them to design a state-of-the-art fighter for the IAF.

The planners at Air Headquarters got to work and issued an Air Staff Target (AST) for a cost-effective replacement for the Ajeet and Mig-21. The aeronautical scientists and engineers did not agree with that approach, and wanted to utilize the opportunity to bridge the technology gap that had opened up between India and the advanced countries of the world since the Marut (HF-24) programme of the 1960s. They wanted the aircraft to have four crucial new technologies which were the fly-by-wire Flight Control System (FCS), a glass cockpit (round dial analogue instruments being replaced by multi-function displays controlled by a mission computer), composite materials in the airframe and micro-processor controlled general systems. They also decided to develop the jet engine to power the LCA as well as a Multi Mode Radar (MMR) which would be the primary sensor on board the aircraft. The seeds for protracted programme delays and cost overruns were sown by these decisions. The IAF not wanting to sound overly pessimistic went along with these ideas, and took the first step of issuing an AST for a multi-role fighter while expressing serious reservations about the development schedule. An AST is a document which contains a preliminary set of operational requirements drawn up by the IAF for discussion with the design agency. During these discussions, designers tell the planning staff at Air HQ whether the operational targets given in the AST can be met with existing technologies available in the country, or whether there would be a need to develop new technologies indigenously, or source them from abroad.

HAL realized they had no experience of working with any of the technologies which had to be incorporated into the new aircraft to meet operational requirement targets set out in the

AST. They were very under-confident of developing an aircraft by the mid-1990s to meet IAF re-equipment plans. They rightly assessed that the programme would require the harnessing of national capabilities across a spectrum of technologies and considerable investment of time and resources towards project management. They felt they were not equal to the task and agreed to the creation of a separate programme management agency.

In 1985 Rajiv Gandhi had become the Prime Minister at the young age of 45 years. An equally young Scientific Adviser to the Raksha Mantri (SA to RM), Dr V.S. Arunachalam, had a grand dream of making DRDO a world class R&D organization. An immediate rapport was established between these two decision makers. Dr Arunachalam became a special favourite of the Prime Minister, but Dr Arunachalam was a metallurgist and not an aeronautical engineer. He quite naturally assumed that anything could be accomplished given the necessary political support, resources, leadership and dedication of the workforce.

Dr Arunachalam was able to prevail upon the GOI to create a Society under the Ministry of Defence called the Aeronautical Development Agency (ADA) to act as the programme management agency for the LCA project. ADA was to be headed by a Director General who would report to the SA to RM. The principal partner in the programme was to be HAL along with other public sector agencies, the private sector and academic institutions. Dr S.R. Valluri, former Director of the National Aerospace Laboratories, was appointed the first Director General of ADA in mid-1985. Dr Valluri was a very renowned aeronautical scientist and commanded much respect in professional circles. He chose Raj Mahindra, former MD of the HAL Design Bureau to be the chief designer of the LCA. They went about putting together a team of designers drawn from ISRO, HAL, NAL and the IAF. A search for a foreign partner was also started, and discussions were held with Dassault Aviation of France, Messerschmitt, Bolkow & Blohm (MBB) of Germany, Dornier of Germany and British Aerospace (now BAE Systems) of the UK. After prolonged discussions at Air HQ, the Ministry of Defence, HAL and the Defence Research and Development Organization (DRDO) an Air Staff Requirement (ASR) for a multi-role fighter was issued by Air HQ in late-1985.

Around this time in late-1985, serious differences emerged between Dr Arunachalam and Dr Valluri over the choice of the chief designer for the project. Dr Arunachalam felt Raj Mahindra was too old to be at the helm of a long gestation project like the design and development of a modern fighter aircraft and wanted a younger man. Dr Valluri refused to relent and resigned from his post. Dr Arunachalam assumed the mantle of DG ADA as well and started looking around for someone in his forties to run the programme. The choice was very limited as there was no one in India who had any experience in managing such a complex undertaking. Finally at the end of 1986, 43-year old Dr Kota Harinarayana who was Director, Aeronautical Development Establishment (ADE) was appointed the Programme Director (LCA), and was for all practical purposes the head of ADA.

Government sanction was received in 1986 to build five prototypes at an estimated cost of about Rs 575 crore. Choosing a foreign collaborator proved difficult, and hectic negotiations were conducted all through 1986. Finally, Dassault Aviation of France was chosen to provide the necessary inputs for the Project Definition Phase (PDP). About 500 HAL Design Bureau engineers were deputed to ADA for the PDP. A dozen aeronautical engineers from Dassault came to Bangalore in July 1987 and got down to work. As all this activity was going on, a debate began about technology choices. The most crucial technology and expertise Indian engineers were interested in, was the fly-by-wire FCS. There was a school of thought which said American FCS technology was the best in the world and the LCA should have nothing less. Another equally strident point of view, which was supported by the IAF, was that the USA was an unreliable source of technology, given its penchant to impose sanctions on countries that did not toe its line of thinking. European sources of technology though not quite up to US standards were far more reliable and therefore India should not go to the USA for the FCS for the LCA. While this debate raged, certain political developments took place which improved Indo-US relations.

Soon after he became the Prime Minister, Rajiv Gandhi went on an official visit to the USA and met President Ronald Reagan for the first time. The leaders of the world's two largest democracies immediately established a good bond between them. When Rajiv Gandhi asked Reagan for help for the LCA programme his request was readily agreed to. The United States Air Force (USAF) was the agency designated to provide help to the Indian DRDO to develop the fly-by-wire FCS. The USAF in turn detailed Wright Laboratories, Dayton, Ohio, to do the needful and the DRDO laboratory chosen to absorb the technology transfer was the Aeronautical Development Establishment (ADE), a DRDO laboratory at Bangalore. The USA also offered to provide GE F-404 jet engines to power the prototypes. This offer was accepted by ADA as everyone knew that the indigenous engine, the Kaveri, would take time to develop, test and certify. In 1987 ADA bought 11 GE F-404 engines at a cost of nearly US$ 11 million.

By the end of 1988 the PDP was completed and the report was circulated to various agencies including Air HQ. The report landed up on the table of Air Commodore S. Krishnaswamy (Kitcha, later CAS), Director Air Staff Requirements. Kitcha was an experienced fighter pilot and a graduate of the Empire Test Pilots School, Boscombe Down, UK.

At that time, in early 1988, he happened to be one of the very few people at Air HQ who understood the nuances of technology choices. He wrote a report on the PDP document, which was very sceptical about ADA's ability to design a state of the art fighter with a host of new technologies, which were being introduced into an aircraft for the first time in the country. He felt, quite rightly, that the time frame projected for design, development including flight testing and introduction into service was far too ambitious. He also said that without foreign help it would be very risky to develop the fly-by-wire system, the glass cockpit, the composite airframe and the micro-processor controlled general systems. Due cognizance was taken of this report by the decision makers at Air HQ. The IAF recommended that a confidence and competence building route of proving the four crucial technologies, by flying two Technology Demonstrator aircraft through a limited flight test programme, be followed before embarking on full-scale engineering development of prototypes.

Dassault Aviation was very keen to partner ADA in the LCA programme and offered the three digital channels with an analogue fourth channel fly-by-wire technology which they had successfully developed for the Rafale fighter. The FCS computer would be a hybrid digi-ana computer having three digital processors with three independent channels and one hard wired analogue channel. In the 1980s confidence in digital technology was not very high, and the French thought it was a good idea to have an analogue channel as a back-up in case of any problems with the digital channels. They said they would go for a quadruplex digital fly-by-wire FCS when they had gained more experience with the digi-ana hybrid FCS.

Unfortunately, their offer was spurned in favour of the quadruplex digital fly-by-wire technology offered by Martin Marietta Control Systems (MMCS), later Lockheed Martin and now BAE Systems of the USA. The FCS computer would be fully digital having four digital processors with four independent channels. The Americans were very confident about the reliability of digital technology and there was no doubt that at that time it was cutting edge technology.

Since they would have no control over the development of a system as crucial as the FCS, Dassault Aviation walked out of the programme, a decision which I am sure both parties regret to this day. With an experienced aircraft house like Dassault as a partner ADA/HAL may well have been able to develop the aircraft, and have it in service by the end of the 1990s. In my view, the decision to accept the US offer of quadruplex digital fly-by-wire technology and go it alone with only consultancy agreements with various foreign firms added a decade or more to the programme. This decision, I suspect, was taken because the thrust was to acquire the latest technology and build self-reliance through indigenization rather than on delivery of an operational fighter in a reasonable time frame to meet IAF modernization plans. It was a classic case of the 'best' being the enemy of the 'good'. Operational requirements should drive technology choices and not the other way around.

At the end of 1989 Rajiv Gandhi lost the general election, and Dr Arunachalam had to establish new equations with the V.P. Singh government. In August 1990, Saddam Hussein of Iraq invaded Kuwait, oil prices sky rocketed and the country's foreign exchange reserves depleted rapidly. The GOI was unable to decide to go ahead with the programme. Two whole years were lost before the programme could be put back on track.

CHAPTER 3

Change of Guard

On 21 May 1991, Rajiv Gandhi was assassinated, even as India's foreign exchange crisis worsened. After elections, a new government was sworn in at the centre headed by P.V. Narasimha Rao and its first and most pressing task was to put the economy back on the rails. The GOI initiated a series of wide ranging economic reforms and introduced austerity measures which included reduced defence expenditure to control the fiscal deficit. Quite naturally the LCA project was put on the low priority list.

In late-1991, Dr Arunachalam handed over the reins of DRDO to Dr A.P.J. Abdul Kalam who, in addition to being SA to the RM, became the third DG, ADA. The LCA programme had carried on with the initial sanction of Rs. 575 crore. The aerodynamic configuration had been frozen and a lot of wind tunnel testing had been conducted at four wind tunnels around the world. No foreign partner had, however, been identified nor was the scope of the project properly defined.

Dr Kalam imparted fresh impetus to the programme and going by the IAF's recommendation, went to the GOI for a sanction of Rs 2188 crore to build two Technology Demonstrator (TD) aircrafts, and prove the four crucial technologies by flying around 220 sorties in a flight test programme. The funding included the building of a structural test specimen as well. The formal go ahead for the TD programme was given by the GOI in June 1993.

In 1992 an agreement was signed with Martin Marietta Control Systems (MMCS) of the USA for assistance to develop the fly-by-wire FCS. Alenia of Italy was chosen to provide the composite wing skins for the first two aircraft. HAL which was to build the prototypes signed up with British Aerospace of UK for assistance to manufacture the wings and to test and integrate the FCS on the airframe. Dr Kalam formed two national teams, one to develop the Control Law (CLAW) for the FCS and the other for the structural design of the composite wings. The CLAW team had personnel drawn from ADA, DRDO, NAL, HAL and the IAF. The wing team had engineers from HAL, ADA and NAL.

The foreign exchange crisis of 1991 forced a decision to go ahead with the indigenous design and development of a number of sub-systems like the Jet Fuel Starter (JFS), a small gas turbine which starts the main engine, and the Aircraft Mounted Auxiliary Gear Box (AMAGB), which transmits main engine power to drive ancillary units like the generator and the hydraulic pumps. The mission computer, display processor, the utilities monitoring system computers, the brake system computer, the entire environmental control system including the cold air unit, some heat exchangers, fuel oil coolers, hydraulic filters and various lights on the aircraft were to be indigenous. This was a daunting task because a number of DRDO labs, PSUs and private sector industries were involved and day-to-day monitoring and coordination was required. Under the dynamic leadership of Dr Kota, Team LCA proved equal to the task and all the items mentioned were indigenized and flew on TD-1 during the first flight. The long lead time required to develop these airworthy items was masked by the time taken to get the FCS ready for flight.

Since flight testing forms an integral part of the development process of an aircraft, ADA signed a Memorandum of Understanding (MOU) with HAL in 1992, to undertake flight testing of the two TD aircraft for the technology demonstration phase. The number of new technologies involved and the extent of indigenization planned before first flight required continuous and in-depth involvement of test pilots and test engineers in the development process. Unfortunately HAL management did not appreciate this requirement, insisting rather, that routine production flight testing should remain the primary job of the two HAL test pilots, and only when they were free of such commitments could they carry out LCA related work. Dr Kota realized early in 1994 that the flight testing MOU with HAL was not working satisfactorily and felt a new solution needed to be found.

I had known Dr Kota from the time when he was the Chief Resident Engineer (CRE) at HAL Nashik in the late 1970s. We had interacted further when he became the Chief Designer at HAL Nashik and I was the Chief Test Pilot (CTP) at the IAF flight test centre, the Aircraft and Systems Testing Establishment (ASTE), Bangalore. In the early 1980s the Nashik Design Bureau had modified a Mig-21 Bis aircraft with a vortex plate which was a sheet metal device bolted on to the leading edge of the wing to reduce drag, additional internal fuel, an enlarged saddle tank, Western avionics and combat flaps. ASTE was tasked to evaluate the efficacy of these modifications. I had flown a number of evaluation sorties on the aircraft and frequently met Dr Kota. In late-1985, Dr Kota became the Director, ADE, at Bangalore, and we were involved in the development of the Kiran and Ajeet flight simulators and other Air Force projects.

At the end of my CTPs tenure in 1988, I was posted out of Bangalore to command the Jaguar base at Gorakhpur, Uttar Pradesh, after which I was lucky enough to be selected to undergo the year-long course at the Royal College of Defence Studies in London, UK, in 1990. The course was the equivalent of that run for Brigadiers and Colonels and equivalent ranks from the sister Services at the National Defence College at New Delhi. It was a marvellous year with plenty of opportunity to interact with officers from 28 different nations including Pakistan. The Crown Prince of Thailand, Lt. Gen. Ravi Mahidol was there as well as Brigadier Pervez Musharraf who later became the President of Pakistan.

On my return to India I was earmarked to take over command of ASTE from AVM A.S. Lamba who was retiring from service at the end of April 1991. During my time as Commandant ASTE, I was given strict instructions by Air HQ not to participate in any LCA related activities with ADA unless specifically authorized by them to do so. I found this particularly galling as I felt the IAF should have removed all restrictions on providing operational inputs to ADA and HAL designers, rather than impose a blanket ban on interaction with the design team.

There was a definite clash of organizational egos between the IAF and DRDO/ADA/HAL. This clash was personality-based and dated back to the start of the project when a decision was taken to go to the Americans for FCS development rather than the French, and the IAF had made its serious misgivings known to the MOD regarding the time frame of the project. Going ahead with the project without proper conflict resolution at this early stage proved to be a weakness which has continued to dog the programme.

As a result of the directive from Air HQ, like a good soldier, I did what I was told to do and attended only those meetings at ADA where I was asked to represent Air HQ or go along with the CAS or DCAS whenever they chose to visit ADA, which was at infrequent intervals. These visits of mine to ADA did have a beneficial effect, in that I became *au fait* with the status of development of various sub-systems including the all-important FCS.

In July 1993 I was posted out of ASTE to Air HQ as the Director, Air Staff Requirements (DASR). In this capacity I had to oversee the LCA project and monitor its progress. One of the first problems I had to deal with was the unsatisfactory state of affairs as far as preparations to flight test the LCA were concerned. After consulting Dr Kota, I suggested the formation of a national flight test team copying the model of the other two national teams which were performing well. I sent this proposal up to my immediate boss AVM S. Krishnaswamy who was the Assistant Chief of the Air Staff (ACAS) Plans at that time.

Thereafter I forgot all about this particular problem.

As the DASR I was tasked with the Mig-21 Bis upgrade project which involved protracted negotiations with Russian designers from the Mikoyan Design Bureau. I led an IAF/HAL/DRDO team for the first round of technical negotiations at Moscow in December 1993. These talks were interesting and fruitful as we were able to decide upon the main technical parameters of the upgrade.

In May 1994, Dr Kota and Dr T.S. Prahalad (Project Director, Technology Development at ADA) came to the DASR's office to see me. They said FCS development was going ahead at a rapid pace and test pilot and flight test engineer involvement in the developmental process was vital. Their view was that it was time a dedicated flight test group started looking at a host of issues like CLAW development which involved development of a real time simulator and extensive flying on it, for assessment of handling qualities, ergonomics of the cockpit, development of failure warning philosophy and display symbology. Normal and emergency operating procedures had to be evolved by the flight test team after in-depth discussions with the designers. Since more than one design agency was involved, continuous involvement with the various design teams over a period of years was required to ensure a safe technology demonstration programme. I appreciated their concern.

They wanted me to agree to be deputed to ADA to be the Project Director, Flight Test, which meant I would be responsible for the flight test programme of the LCA in its entirety. I told them to request Dr Kalam to speak to the CAS, ACM S.K. Kaul, and find out from him whether the IAF was willing to spare my services.

Personally I did not mind the move because I had spent 13 years at ASTE in various capacities, and knew the HAL and DRDO environment very well. As a test pilot and a flight test programme manager of several years standing, I was confident of handling the responsibility. The LCA programme was the largest and most complex aircraft development project ever undertaken in India, and as a flight test specialist I felt it was a good opportunity to make a significant contribution to a national endeavour.

About a month after Dr Kota visited me, I was summoned by the CAS. He said much the same things Dr Kota and Dr Prahalad had told me about the project earlier and I knew what was coming! He said he could think of only two officers in the IAF, Kitcha and I, who had the knowledge and experience to handle this responsibility. He said Kitcha was well placed to become the CAS some day while I was badly placed because I was over a year older than Kitcha and a year junior to him in service. He was not sure that I would even be considered for promotion to the rank of Air Marshal as there were no less then 17 officers ahead of me in the queue. He asked me whether I would be willing to go to ADA on deputation, to head the about-to-be formed National Flight Test Centre (NFTC). I immediately agreed and told the CAS I was confident of handling the assignment.

There was a problem in forming the NFTC as the HAL test pilots were bitterly opposed to the idea of a separate flight test organization being created exclusively for the LCA project. They managed to convince the then Chairman, HAL, Ram Niwas Sharma, that they were the right people to undertake flight testing of the LCA, as HAL was going to build the two Technology Demonstrator aircrafts anyway.

Under normal circumstances their argument was irrefutable.

Unfortunately what HAL did not realize was that the LCA was being developed by DRDO with the involvement of a large number of private Indian agencies and foreign vendors, all of which required excellent coordination and programme management. The new technologies planned to be introduced in the aircraft for the first time in the country required in-depth and continuous involvement of the flight test team with the designers on a day-to-day basis. The job of fabrication of the prototypes and development of the main sub-systems was sub-contracted to HAL. DRDO/ADA wanted to be in the driver's seat for the simple reason that they were the ones who had taken the initiative to go to the GOI for the project sanction. HAL, the premier aircraft development agency, resented being relegated to the position of a junior partner. Though public statements were made at various forums that HAL was an equal partner in the project, the fact was that ADA controlled the project funds, hence the decision-making regarding technology choices and time frames. A lot of ill-feeling was created between the DRDO/ADA and the HAL management, which persists to this day to the incalculable detriment of the project.

At an acrimonious meeting at Air HQ in June 1994, ACM Kaul was able to prevail upon Chairman R.N. Sharma to agree to the formation of the NFTC.

I was promoted to the rank of Air Vice Marshal on 4 July 1994. ACM Kaul called me to his office and put the new rank badges on the epaulettes of my uniform shirt. It was a proud moment for me. I moved from the DASR's office on the fourth floor of Air HQ to the office of the Additional ACAS (Operations) on the fifth floor.

After the hectic pace of work as the DASR, I found my new assignment far less taxing. Fortunately I continued to be involved with the Mig Bis upgrade programme. I led a team to Moscow in July 1994 for the second round of negotiations with the Mikoyan Design Bureau. Follow-up action on our visit took up most of my time for the rest of the month.

The file moved by the personnel branch at Air HQ requesting MOD sanction for my deputation to ADA did its rounds of South Block at glacial speed, while I chafed at the bit to get on with my new assignment. I was finally ordered to report to ADA on 17 September 1994. After the usual flurry of farewell parties, just before I left Delhi for Bangalore I called on the SA, Dr A.P.J. Abdul Kalam who was the person I would be reporting to. He told me in no uncertain terms that there was a lot of bad blood between the IAF, DRDO/ADA and HAL regarding the LCA project. He warned me to tread cautiously and avoid worsening the situation at all costs. He said 'I expect you to play the role of a peacemaker amongst the various groups and win over everyone to the cause of this national project'. With this sage advice ringing in my ears, along with my wife Sheila and daughter Nilima, I headed for Bangalore to begin, what in retrospect, were the most challenging and productive years of my service career.

I will now present the reader a condensed version of my life before I was deputed to ADA.

CHAPTER 4

Early Life and My Career in the IAF

I was born to middle-class parents on 8 August 1941, in the small town of Davangere in the old princely state of Mysore. My father, Dr Clement Somasundaram David was a doctor in the state government medical service and my mother Grace Kamala David was a graduate from St Agnes College, Mangalore. In the India of those years, I was extremely fortunate to have had educated parents who sacrificed a lot to give their children a good education. My parents were not religious in the conventional sense but were morally upright people who inculcated in my two brothers and me the virtues of honesty, hard work and thrift.

My boyhood years were spent in Mysore where my father was posted during his career. I did not go to school till the age of 12, as there was no primary and middle school with English as the medium of instruction. My mother taught both my elder brother and me at home till we were ready to go to high school. As there was no school to attend my brother and I enjoyed our boyhood immensely. Mother would teach us from 9 a.m. till noon, and thereafter we were free birds. We flew kites, played with tops, marbles and the inevitable 'gilli danda'. Tennis ball cricket with two players was another favourite pastime. Father insisted that we should learn swimming, so during the summer, we would walk 4 miles every morning to a big lake to be coached by one of his patients. When my brother started going to high school, he was given a bicycle. Soon I too, learnt to ride one very quickly. Cycles could be hired for two annas per hour (about 12 paise!) and I roamed the streets of our locality enjoying my new-found mobility. Exploration of the whole of Mysore followed thereafter, to the chagrin of my mother who never knew when or where I would disappear on my cycling forays.

Father was posted to Bangalore just after my younger brother was born in September 1953. It was then that I saw a De Havilland Vampire jet fighter screaming across the skies of the city for the first time. Even though I had just entered St Joseph's Indian High School I could not help being fascinated by the thought of piloting that speeding machine. After completing my matriculation I joined the science stream at St Joseph's College, and tried to enrol in the NCC Air Wing to pursue my fast-growing interest in aviation. Alas! I was rejected during selection for being too puny! It was a bitter blow as some of my good friends from school made the grade and I became the object of much friendly pity. The rejection had a beneficial effect, because I joined a gymnasium to improve my physique. Under the watchful eye of my instructor 'Bob' Naidu I added height, weight and muscle to my frame. More importantly Bob made me a life-long fitness addict and I never had a problem with medical examinations during my subsequent career in the IAF.

I started hearing from my NCC friends about their progress in drill and aero-modelling. I could only listen to their exploits. I had no problems with college level physics, maths and chemistry, and I spent every spare minute reading about flying. World War II books about the Battle of Britain and Paul Brickhill's books *Reach for the Sky* about the legless Royal Air Force fighter pilot Douglas Bader, and the *Dam Busters* were special favourites. Aircraft had started flying faster than sound and the age of supersonic flight had arrived. Tales of test pilots breaking the sound barrier at the famous Farnborough air show in the UK and the Californian desert, made me long to be 'up there' with them. In the 1950s Bangalore had a gliding club at Jakkur, about 10 miles north of the city on the road to the present-day Yelahanka air base. When my friends started flying gliders training I began cycling there on Saturday afternoons to watch them go up with their instructor in a two-seater glider. A glider launch by a winch cost Re 1 and the glider would stay up in the air for about 3–4 minutes. By saving my pocket money I was able to do a few launches with an instructor and the sheer exhilaration of being airborne made me make up my mind to become a fighter pilot in the IAF.

At the end of two years in college, it was time to join a professional course like medicine or engineering. Those careers did not interest me as I wanted to fly jet fighters in the IAF. I was already past the age to enter the National Defence Academy at Khadakvasala and the only option open to me was to appear for the Union Public Service Commission examination for direct entry to the Air Force Flying College (AFFC) at Jodhpur. If I had joined a professional course, my parents would never have allowed me to have a crack at the examination. Resisting parental pressure, especially from my father, I joined the two year B.Sc. degree course at Central College, Bangalore, again with Physics, Mathematics and Chemistry as the major subjects. I graduated in April 1960, ending my seven years in the formal education stream and appeared for the entrance examination at the end of the year. I was selected to undergo flying training at the AFFC Jodhpur with the 82nd Pilot's Course from 1 July 1961. When the course commenced, I was a month short of my twentieth birthday. My father gave me some advice before I left home. He said 'Son, in life you will get opportunities to make money by unfair means. Do not do it. If you do, please do not come back here'. He passed away at the grand old age of 93 in June 1998, two years after I became an Air Marshal. I never forgot his advice throughout my career.

At the AFFC we flew two piston-engined propeller-driven trainers, 50 hours on the HT-2 manufactured by HAL during the first six months and 75 hours on the North American T-6G Texan later. In addition to flying training, we were taught subjects like meteorology, navigation, principles of flight, airframes, aero engines, flying instruments, aircraft general systems, administration, Air Force law and Hindi. We also spent a lot of time on the drill square, sports field and the swimming pool. The training was hectic as the day started at 6 a.m. and except for very short breaks continued till 'lights out' at 10 p.m. Saturday afternoons and Sundays were free when we caught up with sleep and written assignments. Strict discipline was enforced by both flying and ground instructors but it was never harsh. Many cadets did not make the grade in flying and the number dwindled from 80 at the start of the course to about 50 by the time we left Jodhpur. After the first year we were split into two streams, one for fighter training at the Jet Training Wing, Hakimpet, Secunderabad, and the other for transport training at the Transport Training Wing, Begumpet, Secunderabad. I was lucky to get my request to be sent for fighter training approved because my flying instructor had recommended me for transports. I was absolutely thrilled when I went solo in a Vampire fighter, the same type which I had seen over Bangalore as a lad. While we were at JTW, the border conflict with China started on 20 October 1962 and 45 of us from both training streams were awarded 'Wings' and commissioned as Pilot Officers in the IAF on 10 November 1962, about six weeks earlier than scheduled. We continued our training at JTW and at the end of February 1963, were posted to operational fighter squadrons.

I landed up in No. 47 Squadron, equipped with Toofanis, at Kalaikunda in West Bengal. Conversion on to the Toofani, an early product of Dassault Aviation of France, was followed by a more demanding operational training syllabus. The squadron moved to Bagdogra, which is at the foot of the Darjeeling hills, in August 1963, our living conditions being rather primitive. Two officers had to share a 180 pounder tent and the torrential rains in the Terai region of North Bengal made life pretty uncomfortable, but all these minor irritants were forgotten once we got into the air! Squadron flying was great fun as one was constantly learning from the senior pilots and from one's own mistakes. I also met some great guys like Satish Inamdar (later Air Marshal, Vice Chief of the Air Staff) in the squadron who became a close friend.

Following the border war with China, Pandit Nehru had appealed to President Kennedy for help to speedily improve the state of the Indian Armed Forces as our weaknesses had been glaringly exposed by that short war. The United States Air Force (USAF) had agreed to provide gunnery training to about 70 pilots who had not been declared 'Fully Operational' on a front line fighter. As soon as I had 200 jet hours in my log book and an instrument rating (a pilot is tested for his ability to fly by only looking at his flying instruments without any visual reference and awarded a rating), I was on my way to the USA in April 1964. After tent life in Bagdogra landing up in a USAF base was a culture shock! Everything looked spick and span and there was an air of great efficiency. Gleaming cars and pretty girls seemed to be everywhere! After five months in the USA, including three months in the gambling capital of the world, Las Vegas, during which I flew 50 hours on the T-33A jet trainer and 25 hours on the F-86-F fighter of Korean war fame, I returned to India in September 1964, immeasurably richer in skills and confidence. After debriefing at Air HQ, I was posted to No 1 'Tiger' Squadron, equipped with the Dassault Mystere IVA ground attack fighter, at Adampur, close to Jullundur in Punjab. The squadron was commanded by Wing Commander Om Prakash 'Omi' Taneja. A fighter squadron is divided into two flights of eight aircraft each, and Omi's Flight Commanders were Squadron Leader (Sqn. Ldr.) Patrick Russel 'Paddy' Earle and Sqn. Ldr. Denzil 'Denny' Satur.

The Mystere IVA could exceed the speed of sound in a dive and on 12 October 1964, I broke the sound barrier 17 years after Chuck Yeager had done so for the first time ever over the skies of California, in his experimental rocket powered aircraft, the Bell X-1.

It was a huge thrill! Operational flying training in the squadron progressed rapidly and when the Indo-Pak war started on 1 September 1965, I was fully operational and ready for the fray.

For the first five days only the Mystere and Gnat squadrons

based at Pathankot to the North of Adampur saw action in the Chamb sector while we chafed at the bit. No 1 Squadron was sent into action at dawn on 6 September 1965. After the first search and strike mission in the Gujranwala sector led by Omi Taneja, nothing happened for the rest of the morning. At 1 p.m. we heard Field Marshal Ayub Khan, President of Pakistan, telling his countrymen on Radio Pakistan that the Indian Army had committed aggression by crossing the international border in the Sialkot, Dera Baba Nanak and Lahore sectors, and that Pakistan had no option but to defend itself. We anxiously waited for orders to go into action but none came.

Around 5 p.m. we heard the news that Pathankot airfield had been raided by the Pakistan Air Force (PAF) and that a number of our aircraft had been destroyed on the ground. As dusk fell we were told to go back to the mess. My room mate 'Frisky' Verma (later Air Marshal, AOC-in-C, Central Air Command), and I got on to Frisky's Jawa motorbike and set-off for the mess when there was a loud explosion at the Southern end of the runway and the anti-aircraft guns opened fire. Glowing red balls of tracer shells arced through the fading light and in their glow I picked out the silhouette of a PAF B-57 bomber go past. I yelled 'Frisky, B-57 over us' and we dived into a trench. The Pak bomber carried out a second attack and dropped a bomb near the Air Traffic Control (ATC) building at the middle of the 3000 yard runway. After about 15 minutes the all clear sounded and we gingerly rode back to the mess in pitch darkness because black out had been enforced not only in the base but all over Punjab. In the mess pilots from the other two Mystere squadrons on the base and a number of senior flying instructors from Training Command who had been attached to the three squadrons for operational duties were gathered in little knots, talking in hushed notes about another PAF raid on Halwara to the south of us, earlier that evening. Some more bad news came in of a Mig-21 parked at the end of our runway being destroyed by the PAF bomber. The only cheery news was that two F-86F Sabre jets of the

PAF had been shot down by our Hunter fighters over Halwara. We all knew that the IAF would have to retaliate the next day but we had no idea of where and when. Paddy Earle came to the mess and told all of us to have an early dinner and catch some sleep. I slept fitfully, rolling and tossing in bed not knowing what to expect. We were woken up by a messenger at 3 a.m. and told to report to the squadron briefing room at 4 a.m. No mission details were given and we could only guess that it was something big.

When we assembled in the briefing room fitted with black out curtains, I looked at the briefing board and saw the formation details for a 12 aircraft attack on Sargodha, the heavily defended PAF base, about 100 miles inside Pakistan. As my eyes ran over the details my heart sank because I saw Frisky's name in the first wave of four aircraft but did not see my name. I was going to miss all the action! Another frantic search and I found my name at No. 12 in the list, in the last wave of four—I was to be 'tail end Charlie'. As enemy aircraft attempting to intercept our formation would have to approach from the rear to bring their forward firing guns to bear on our aircraft, the job of the last man in the formation, was to warn the others about an impending attack. The job required the keen eyes of a hawk and a rubber neck to keep looking as far back as possible. It was a crucial duty and I had been chosen to do it. My disappointment gave way to pride. It could have also meant that I was disposable but I preferred the earlier thought! Two senior flying instructors, one of them Sqn. Ldr. A.B. Devayya, were stand bys, in case any of the first 12 aircraft dropped out.

Omi Taneja started the briefing with a serious demeanour. The excitement and tension in the room was palpable. This was the real thing! We had to start up and taxi out to the take-off point in the correct sequence in total radio silence on unlit taxi tracks. The runway lights would come only when we were ready to roll. Take-off would be in pairs with each aircraft occupying one half of the runway, while the interval between pairs was to be 30 seconds, to avoid the jet wake of the aircraft in front. We were to take off at 5.28 a.m. and fly at 300 ft Above Ground Level (AGL) in darkness for 30 minutes and carry out our attacks at 30 second intervals at 5.58 a.m. just as dawn was breaking over the target. The very low altitude was chosen for the inbound leg to avoid radar detection. Navigation would be only by compass and stop watch, as darkness would not permit map reading. Omi would lead the first four aircraft armed with eight T-10 rockets each, Denny Satur the second four armed with thirty-six SNEB 68 mm rockets each, and Sqn. Ldr. Sudarshan Handa the last four with two 1000 pound bombs each. As the target was at the extreme distance the Mystere could go at a height of 300 ft AGL with a full fuel and armament load, we had to fly at the optimum speed for range which was about 120 mph slower than the preferred tactical speed for manoeuvring at low level. Each of the 12 pilots was given a specific target to attack on the airfield with preference for aircraft spotted on the airfield.

We synchronized watches and the briefing ended at 5 a.m. Some biscuits and tea had been served during the briefing by junior pilots who were not part of the formation. I loaded my revolver and stuffed it into my flying suit along with some Pakistani currency. These items were to facilitate escape in case of being shot down! I picked up my back parachute and flying helmet and checked that everything was in order. Dry-mouthed, I started walking in the inky night to the pen where my aircraft was parked when the air raid siren went off and the anti-aircraft guns started to fire the by now familiar red tracer shells. It was a clear starlit sky and I picked out a moving pinpoint of light overhead and immediately realized it was a passing satellite at a height of a couple of hundred miles, but our gunners did not know that! They kept up a barrage of fire for a few minutes. I jumped into a nearby trench and waited for the all clear to sound when I heard Omi's aircraft, which was parked close to where my aircraft was, start up. I flashed the torch on my watch and it was already 5.18 a.m., only 10 minutes to go for take off! I ran to my aircraft, climbed into the cockpit, started the engine and while it was revving up I strapped up and caught up with the other 11 aircraft which were ghostly shapes on the taxi track. Omi and his four aircraft lined up and took off on time followed by Denny and his four. As Handa rolled on to the runway followed by his wingman Flt. Lt. Darshan Singh Brar, I saw the two standby aircraft with their engines running parked to one side of the take-off point. My sub-section leader Flt. Lt. Dilmohan Singh 'Kay' Kahai took up position behind Handa and Handa began his take off. I suddenly saw one of the standby pilots, Sqn. Ldr. Devayya, move on to the runway and begin rolling in front of Kay. The second bomb dropped by the PAF B-57 the previous night had exploded to one side of the runway about 1500 yards from where we began rolling. A lot of mud was lying on the runway and the jet wake of the preceding aircraft had created a dense dust cloud. As I raised the nose wheel at about 140 mph, I entered the dust cloud and lost all visual reference. After about three or four seconds I emerged from the cloud ready to lift off when I saw this enormous Mystere filling my front windshield. Devayya, who had no business to be in the formation as no one had dropped out, had drifted into my half of the runway and I was about to collide with him! Fortunately for me the Mystere had a characteristic, which I knew about, of yawing to the right if one attempted to get it off the ground before it was ready to fly off on its own. I did exactly that and the heavily laden aircraft yawed and staggered into the air. I quickly raised the wheels to reduce drag, concentrating on staying in the air. The aircraft accelerated slowly and after what seemed an eternity I had things under control but I had lost sight of Kay's aircraft.

I headed north-west for the Beas river bridge, in the hope of spotting the formation but it was an impossible task in the darkness, as all aircraft were flying with their navigation lights switched off. I consumed fuel and returned to base with my bombs. About 20 minutes after I landed the formation returned. Devayya was missing and Handa's formation had missed the target due to a navigational error in the darkness and had returned to base with their bomb load.

At the debriefing Omi Taneja was unhappy. He ordered Handa's formation to attack Sargodha in broad daylight at 9.45a.m.! This was a most unexpected order because there would be no cover of darkness for the inbound leg and the alerted defences would give us a hearty reception. The chances of being intercepted by enemy fighters and shot down were very bright but orders were orders and we had to obey.

After breakfast, Handa went over the briefing once again and Brar, Kay and I listened in stony silence. Since the attack would be in daylight we were given specific targets picked out from an aerial photograph taken by a reconnaissance aircraft some years earlier. We were to carry out a shallow glide bombing attack releasing the bombs at about 800 ft AGL and pulling out by 200 ft AGL. To avoid being damaged by the exploding bombs at such a low height, the bombs were fitted with 20 second-delay fuses to give adequate time for the aircraft to get clear.

I had butterflies in my stomach, as we walked to our aircraft because I was only 24 years old and did not want to die! Once in the cockpit all fear vanished because one became busy running through a host of checks and procedures which required the utmost concentration. It was a cloudless, sunny day with unlimited visibility and we took off at 9.45 a.m., planning to be over target at 10.15 a.m. After take-off we formed up in low-level tactical formation. Handa was in front with Kay about 1000 yards to his right. Brar and I were behind and to the outside of the leaders at a distance of 200 yards. This way, Brar could look to his right and clear the area behind me, to spot any approaching fighters and I could do the same for him, by looking left. As we crossed the international border, I saw Brar's gun ports winking as he fired a short burst to check that his guns were working. I checked my gun sight and did the same, as Handa descended to about 100 ft AGL. I kept looking behind Brar all the time but did not spot any enemy aircraft. Fuel consumption was as planned. We hit the railway line about 20 miles to the north-east of the target and Handa turned left to follow the railway line to Sargodha. This offered the briefed moment to open full power, accelerate to tactical speed and turn on the armament switches.

Two minutes later, Handa's call 'Pulling up' came over the radio and all four of us eased up to 2500 ft and rolled into a shallow dive to the left in a south-easterly direction. As we settled into the dive I saw the Sargodha runway for the first time and rapidly scanned the skies all around for enemy aircraft. After ensuring that there was no immediate threat to the formation I tried to identify my target which was a missile dump to the south of the runway. The four aircraft were now strung out in a line with Handa in front, and me at the top of the dive about 1500 yards behind him. I saw a bright orange flash on the ground at the northern end of the runway and Handa yelled 'Aircraft at end of the runway'. After dropping his bombs on a bulk petroleum installation to the north of the runway Handa had spotted four aircraft, three F-86F Sabres and one F-104 Starfighter parked on the Operational Readiness Platform (ORP) at the northern end of the runway. He had opened fire with his guns blowing up a Sabre with his burst. I shouted 'Sir, you got him' and saw black puffs dot the sky in our dive direction. The anti-aircraft guns of Sargodha had opened up. Since I was aiming to drop my bombs on the briefed target at the south of the runway, I was not able to point my guns at that juicy target. I released my bombs and fired my guns at what appeared to be aircraft standing on the southern ORP but there was no explosion, indicating they were decoys. During my bombing dive I had lost sight of the other aircraft and as I pulled out of my dive at barely 100 ft AGL, I saw Handa's aircraft on the horizon with Brar to his left. Brar called out, 'Bogey (unidentified aircraft) left 8'o clock high'. I looked to my left, saw only black puffs and called out that it was flak (anti-aircraft shell bursts).With the bombs gone and the drop tanks empty, I was now at 500 mph at less than 100 ft AGL when I saw Kay to my left. Handa called out 'Confirm all with me' and I replied 'All with you, sir'.

Now the fuel problem started because we had calculated fuel consumption at full throttle for only two minutes during the get away, but because of Brar's call Handa maintained full power for almost eight minutes. While still deep inside Pakistan my remaining fuel was considerably less than the planned figure. I reported this to Handa and he eased back on the throttle. We were flying really low and fast at this time because I could see the jet wake from Handa's aircraft cutting a swathe over the standing crop in the fields we were flying over. We must have been no more than 50 ft AGL, and we maintained this height till we crossed the border. According to standard practice, I maintained a height of about 30 ft above the leader's aircraft to be able to concentrate on my look-out duties. When we were flying to the north of Lahore I saw a glint in the sky above and to the left of the formation. It could only have come from a turning aircraft and I reported, 'Bogey, left 7 o'clock' high' and Handa called out 'Buster' which meant opening full power. As we crossed the border my low fuel red warning light came on in the cockpit indicating a fuel reserve of about 10 minutes at the engine power I was using and I reported this to Handa. He replied 'You are over India now and you can eject if you have to'. I had no intention of doing that, and we unintentionally flew over the radar unit at Amritsar. Our own anti-aircraft guns started firing at us and I saw the red tracer shells coming straight at me and then burning out. Fortunately no one was hit and I called out that I was easing up to 6000 ft AGL to spot Adampur. To my relief I saw the runway from a distance of about 15 miles. I throttled back, descended to traffic pattern height, did a tight pattern and touched down with barely three minutes of fuel left in my tanks.

Back in the crew room every one clustered around us to hear about the results of our raid. When I announced that Handa had destroyed a Sabre on the ground a cheer went up. Kay had dropped his bombs on the other aircraft at the northern ORP and Brar had dropped his bombs on an aircraft hangar. We had no idea what damage our bombs had caused because there was no post-raid reconnaissance to assess the damage. Ours was the most successful mission of the entire day because we had returned unscathed from the enemy's lair after destroying an aircraft and some installations on the ground. Handa's formation had redeemed itself in style after the early morning mistakes! I grabbed a cup of tea, sat down and noticed that my hands were shaking. The 90-minute adrenalin rush was over!

That night there were reports that Pakistan had dropped some infiltrators by parachute around the airfields in Punjab including Adampur. We were called back to the squadron and spent the entire night guarding our precious aircraft, while a furious gunfight went on between our squadron airmen and an enemy who was returning the fire from behind the fields adjoining the airfield perimeter. When dawn broke we were bleary eyed not having slept a wink all night. A search of the fields behind the squadron did not reveal any intruders. It turned out that our fire was being returned by our own airmen in the Mechanical Transport section which was located behind the fields. We had spent the whole night firing at each other! I can never forget the events of 7 September 1965.

In 1980, the PAF admitted to an English journalist that they had lost a F-104 Starfighter in combat with a Mystere during the dawn raid by the Tigers on 7 September 1965. Both aircraft had engaged in a dogfight at low level and shot each other down. The Starfighter pilot had ejected and survived but the Mystere pilot had gone down with his aircraft. As no one else had claimed this 'kill', the aircraft could have been shot down only by Devayya. Air HQ doggedly pursued this case with the Ministry of Defence and on 26 January 1988 more than 22 years after the event Devayya was awarded a posthumous Maha Vir Chakra for his act of bravery which has ensured him a hallowed niche in the pantheon of Indian air warriors.

I flew 14 more missions before a ceasefire was declared on 22 September 1965. Seven of these missions were in support of the Indian Army in the Lahore sector, while the rest were armed patrols over our territory. During one of the army support missions I picked up a small-arms bullet in my right wing. It had passed clean through the wing fuel tank which was fortunately empty at that moment, but none of these missions matched the high voltage drama of the Sargodha raid. On 17 September 1965 I was promoted to the rank of Flight Lieutenant, and in November 1966. I was awarded a Mention-in-Despatches for gallantry during the operations.

During this short conflict I learnt a real lesson in leadership. For almost the entire year preceding the war, we young pilots never saw our Commanding Officer, Omi Taneja. He hardly flew with us, came late to work, disappeared in the afternoons to Jullundur Club where, rumour had it, he was courting a beautiful lady. On the other hand the second Mystere squadron CO was always with his 'boys', flying, playing cricket or downing beers on Saturday afternoons. We were quite envious of the camaraderie we saw in their squadron. However, when hostilities were about to break out there was a dramatic change in Omi Taneja. He flew a few sorties and led the very first mission across the border. Thereafter, he led the dawn attack on Sargodha and flew several more missions never exhibiting the slightest trace of anxiety or fear. There was absolutely no doubt in anyone's mind that he was the 'Boss'. He became an instant source of inspiration for all of us young pilots. Wartime leadership is all about leading from the front in the face of the enemy, and Omi certainly did that. As for the 'peacetime' CO across the runway, he never flew a single operational mission during the war and was removed from command!

The following year saw No. 1 Squadron being re-equipped with Mig-21 aircraft of Soviet origin, and I converted to that type with the rest of the squadron pilots. The Mig-21 was a high-performance aircraft which could climb to 63,000 ft like a homesick angel, accelerating to twice the speed of sound in a matter of minutes. It was quite a demanding machine to master and was equipped with a nose-mounted radar using which, it was possible to intercept intruding aircraft by day and night. We did a lot of flying by night, practising interceptions with radar controllers on the ground. During practice interceptions a pair of aircraft would take off and one aircraft would be designated the 'target' and the other the 'fighter'. The fighter would be directed by the ground radar controller to a position from where, with the help of its own radar it could 'launch' an air-to-air missile at the 'target'. For the second interception the roles would be reversed. Landing the Mig-21 on a moonless night on a runway marked with only kerosene flares and no other approach aids like the Precision Approach Path Indicator (PAPI) was hair raising, because of the high rate of descent on the final approach to landing and poor forward visibility from the cockpit. Normal civil airliners descend at about 800 ft per minute while the Mig-21 came down at 2000 ft per minute! The skill required to reduce this high rate of descent and pull off a reasonable landing was considerable, requiring intense concentration. Fortunately for a 25-year old such challenges were an enjoyable experience! I flew as much as I could every month and soon became fully operational on the aircraft. At the end of 1969, I married Sheila D'Souza, a girl from Bangalore and we set-up our first home in Adampur.

The IAF top brass had long wanted to set up a 'Top Gun' school for fighter pilots and finally in February 1971, the Tactics and Combat, Development and Training Squadron (T&C, D&TS) was formed at Adampur. This unit later became the Tactics and Combat Development Establishment (TACDE). By this time I was the second-most experienced Mig-21 pilot in the IAF with four continuous years of above the average flying assessments by my Commanding Officers, in my log book. Based on my track record I was posted to this prestigious training squadron as an instructor. Around the same time I was earmarked by the Personnel branch at Air HQ to undergo training as an experimental test pilot at the French Test Pilots School at Istres (near Marseille), France later that year. By October 1971, war clouds were again gathering over the sub-continent and our training squadron was given an operational task to carry out single aircraft night harassment raids over Pakistan Air Force airfields. I was training to visit Sargodha again by night, when I got my orders to go to

France in the second week of October 1971. I, therefore, missed seeing action during the December 1971 war.

Test pilot training had a lot of technical content and was conducted entirely in French! A refresher course in college level maths and physics was followed by courses in thermodynamics, aerodynamics, mechanics of flight, aircraft structures, flight test techniques, handling qualities of aircraft, flight test instrumentation, fly-by-wire flight control systems, aircraft general systems, inertial navigation systems, communication systems, radar systems and the theory of piston, turbojet and turboprop engines. Each capsule was followed by a written as well as an oral test. One had to work very hard to cope with 120 hours of flying on 16 different types of aircraft, including transports, and 400 hours of ground lectures in a foreign language. Reading and writing French in the class room was quite different from understanding and executing instructions given in French by a radar controller, bringing one down for landing in a Mirage III fighter, under poor visibility conditions. A wrong interpretation of instructions could have spelt disaster! I worked really hard to complete the course as the ground subjects' tests and flying tests were never ending, and having to manage in a language I was not fluent in did not make it any easier. On my return to India in July 1972 with the coveted 'Brevet de Pilote d'Essais' (test pilot's wings) I was posted to the Aircraft and Systems Testing Establishment (ASTE) at Kanpur and promoted to the rank of Sqn. Ldr. ASTE moved to Bangalore in June1973, and a month later our daughter, Nilima, was born.

I spent a total of 13 years at ASTE in five different postings, including four years as the Chief Test Pilot (CTP), and two years and two months as the Commandant of the Establishment. During my years at ASTE I participated in development flight trials of a large number of indigenously-developed aircraft, armament and airborne systems. I carried out prototype test-flying on the Kiran MK I and MK II trainers, HF-24 Marut trainer, Ajeet fighter and trainer, Hindustan Piston Trainer-32 (HPT-32), Hindustan Turbo Trainer-34

(HTT-34) and the Avro 748 twin engine turbo prop pilot trainer. India had embarked on a programme to attain self-sufficiency in conventional weapons like bombs and missiles. I took part in weapon development testing of the Armament Research and Development Establishment (ARDE) developed 1000 pound retarder bomb, cluster bomb, runway penetrator bomb and a target missile for air-to-air missile firing. The Jaguar strike aircraft was inducted into the IAF at end of the 1970s, and I participated in development flight trials of the DARIN second generation Nav/Attack system for this aircraft. In addition to participating in flight tests I was the flight test programme manager for four years, till Final Operational Clearance (FOC) was issued for the system. This was followed by development flight trials of the Self-Protection Jammer (SPJ) Electronic Warfare (EW) pod on the Jaguar. In early 1987, development flight trials of the Maritime Jaguar were carried out only at ASTE, as no other nation had asked for an air-to-sea radar to be mounted in the nose of the aircraft. This required the nose to be modified with side-mounted air data probes to accommodate the radar. The pressure error correction for these probes, handling qualities with the modified nose shape and radar performance were tested and documented. I was the project pilot for this programme. In late 1987, I was specially tasked by Air HQ to modify a Jaguar fighter and carry out over wing R-60 CCM missile firing trials. From go ahead, these trials were completed in three months within the Air HQ allotted modification budget of Rs 25,000! Prototype flight testing of an Avro 748 equipped with a 24-foot rotodome involving initial envelope expansion, slow speed handling, stalling, single engine handling and performance were executed by me for the indigenous Airborne Early Warning programme.

During prototype development of the HPT-32 trainer, a dispute arose between the IAF and HAL in 1980 about the acceptability of the spinning characteristics of the aircraft. I was a member of the Air Marshal C.V. Gole committee, which was constituted by Air HQ to resolve the problem. After a large number of spin tests on the aircraft with HAL and IAF pilots, we were able to clear the aircraft for induction into service. In 1984 Air HQ nominated me as the team leader of a 12-member Air Force/Army team to carry out service induction trials of the AN-32 transport aircraft. This involved trial landings at forward airfields like Mechuka, Tuting and Walong in Arunachal Pradesh and Leh and Thoise in Ladakh, followed by para-dropping trials of men and material at Agra. The stalling characteristics of the aircraft with the new double-slotted flaps also had to be investigated. Along with the Antonov test pilot, Katchienko, I carried out a number of stalls in level and turning flight in various configurations, to investigate stall behaviour. The AN-32 performed very well in all these trials and was inducted into service in late-1984. In all I carried out over a 100 service trials at ASTE.

I was a test pilot in IAF evaluation teams sent for evaluation of the Sukhoi 22 swing-wing fighter in the Soviet Union in 1973, R-13F jet engine for the Mig-21 in the Soviet Union in 1975, Mig-23 BN swing-wing ground attack aircraft in the Soviet Union in 1979, Alpha Jet Advanced Jet Trainer (AJT) in France in 1986, Hawk AJT in the UK in 1986 and a Mig-21 modified with a Nav/Attack System in Egypt in 1987.

In 1991 when I was Commandant ASTE, Air HQ made me the leader of a Tri Service team set-up to evaluate and plan the induction into service of the indigenous Pilotless Target Aircraft (PTA) designed and developed by ADE, a DRDO laboratory. This team was called the Joint Trials Panning and Evaluation Group (JTPEG). I went with the team to the Chandipur-on-sea test range in Orissa, to evaluate the performance of the target, system over a period of two weeks and recommended some improvements before induction into service. With these improvements in place the PTA is being used by all the three Services today.

I have listed some of the work I did to give the reader an idea of how varied and interesting life was at ASTE. Every day posed a new professional or managerial challenge and I enjoyed myself hugely. In addition this was invaluable experience, because one got a good feel for Indian capability to design and develop aircraft and systems.

Apart from test flying duties I had the opportunity to play a significant role in setting up the Test Pilots School (TPS) at ASTE. I became the second Commanding Officer (CO) of the TPS in June 1975, did two more tenures as the CO in 1980–1 and 1983–4. and did a lot of instructional flying with student test pilots. I have in my log book a prized certificate signed by Air Cmde R.D. Sahni, Commandant, ASTE in 1976 authorizing me to impart dual instruction on the Kiran, Hunter trainer, Mig-21 trainer, Marut trainer, Canberra trainer and Avro 748. I believe I am the only test pilot in the IAF to have been officially cleared to instruct on six different types of aircraft at one time. As I had never done the All Purpose Flying Instructors Course at the Flying Instructors School at Tambaram, it was a great experience for me. I was an Instrument Rating Examiner on the Avro 748 and Mig-21 aircraft for over a decade. Today the TPS has grown to include the training of rotary wing test pilots, Flight Test Engineers (FTEs) and Flight Test Instrumentation Engineers (FTIEs). This has made India self-sufficient for all flight test crew requirements for both fixed and rotary wing aircraft. International recognition was received in 2005, when the Society of Experimental Test Pilots (SETP) of the USA recognized it as one of the six schools in the world which imparts training to global standards. It was my good fortune to have been associated with this fine institution during its formative years.

In between these stints at ASTE, I attended a year-long course at the Defence Services Staff College (DSSC) at Wellington, Tamil Nadu in 1976. I did my Flight Commander's tenure in 3 Sqn under Wg. Cdr. D.R. 'Natty' Nadkarni in 1977–8 and had the satisfaction of seeing the squadron being awarded the IAF Flight Safety Trophy for 1978, for having completed 3000 hours of accident-free flying during that year. I completed the Fighter Combat Leader's course at the TACDE, was promoted to Wg. Cdr. and commanded a Mig-21 squadron (1978–80). I was also lucky to be deputed to the

Iraqi Air Force for two years as a Mig-21 fighter combat instructor (1981–3). I became a Group Captain in 1984 and an Air Commodore in 1988. After my first tenure of three and a half years at ASTE I was awarded the Vayu Sena Medal (VM) and after my CTP's tenure of four years I was awarded the Ati Vishisht Seva Medal (AVSM).

CHAPTER 5

The Aeronautical Development Agency

Dr Kota greeted me warmly when I reported to ADA on 17 September 1994. I told him I would work closely with him on the day-to-day progress of the project but I would not be reporting to him as my reporting officer would be the DG ADA, Dr Kalam. In other words Dr Kalam would write my annual confidential report and forward it to the Deputy Chief of the Air Staff at Air HQ. I had earlier insisted on this reporting arrangement as I was senior in government service to Dr Kota and more importantly wanted my independence from the Programme Director as I would be finally responsible for flight safety when flight testing actually began. Dr Kota readily agreed to this arrangement.

At this stage of my narrative, I must describe the LCA Technology Demonstrator (TD) aircraft to the reader. The TD was designed as a single seat, single engine, tailless delta wing aircraft with a target empty weight of six tons. It would have compound (double) sweep of the leading edge and a swept back fin making it capable of supersonic flight. The flying controls would consist of two pairs of elevons (inboard and outboard) at the trailing edge of the wing, leading edge slats, a rudder and airbrakes. A tricycle undercarriage (two main wheels and one nose wheel) would be provided. The power plant chosen for the TD aircraft was the US-made General Electric F404 F2J3 engine of 80 kilo Newtons thrust with afterburner. The Flight Control System (FCS) would be a quadruplex digital fly-by-wire system. The wings would be made of carbon composite material and the cockpit would be 'glass', meaning that information required to pilot the aircraft would be displayed on Multi Function Displays (MFDs) driven by a Mission Computer. The FCS and the 'glass' cockpit were to be developed by ADA/DRDO. The airframe and utility systems on the aircraft like hydraulics, electrics, fuel, environmental control, undercarriage and brakes were to be indigenously designed and manufactured by HAL (AR&DC).

After finishing arrival formalities, I went to the prototype hangar at HAL (Bangalore Complex) and found the first Technology Demonstrator (TD-1) aircraft's fuselage under construction. The noise of the rivet guns was deafening and I beat a hasty retreat to my new office wondering whether I would ever see it fly!

My first task was to assemble a team of flight test personnel drawn from the IAF, HAL, and ADA. The HAL test pilots Wg. Cdr. Rakesh Sharma (India's first Cosmonaut), and Sqn. Ldr. Baldev Singh along with Sqn. Ldr. Uday Shankar of ASTE were at the British Aerospace (BAe) simulation facility at Warton, UK, assessing the first version of the control law (CLAW) developed by the National Control Law Team. They were therefore, automatic choices.

I had to pick a test pilot to join the two HAL test pilots who were working in the programme. Wg. Cdr. Rajiv Kothiyal, a Mig-29 pilot, had undergone the Experimental Test Pilots course at the United States Air Force (USAF) Test Pilots School at Edwards Air Force Base, California in 1990. I was aware of his flying skills and high level of maturity as he had worked with me when I was Commandant ASTE in 1991–3. His training had been paid for out of LCA project funds. He had heard of my move to ADA and met me when I was still the DASR at Air HQ. He told me he was very keen to make use of this once in a lifetime opportunity, to participate in a prototype development programme. I had no hesitation in choosing him as the third test pilot (TP) in the programme.

Sqn. Ldr. Uday Shankar was a Flight Test Engineer (FTE) who had also been trained at the USAF Test Pilots School in 1991 out of LCA project funds. As he was already working with the HAL TPs in the UK for CLAW evaluation, I had no difficulty in getting him into NFTC.

I still needed at least two more FTEs at NFTC, one from the mechanical stream, and the other from the electronics stream, who would look after instrumentation and data acquisition tasks on the TDs. I rang up Wg. Cdr. P.K. Raveendran, a French trained FTE who was at the Base Repair Depot at Sulur, Coimbatore, and asked him whether he would like to be involved in some true experimental testing work. He said he would be thrilled to get this rare opportunity to work in a prototype programme, and came to NFTC.

For the instrumentation work I chose Wg. Cdr. Sudhakar Kunte who was a Flight Test Instrumentation Engineer (FTIE) who had been trained at the ASTE Test Pilots School in the mid-1980s. He had worked with me earlier at ASTE and I knew he was a thorough professional. He was to work closely with Shri Sudham Hanamanth, instrumentation engineer at the fixed wing Flight Test Centre of HAL (BC).

There had to be a team to analyse the vast amount of flight test data which would be acquired during flight testing, and for this work I requested Dr Kota to give me three engineers from ADA. Shri Nalte, Shri Gautamski Vohra and Shri Kamini Kantha Mohapatra came over to the NFTC. Though all were qualified aeronautical engineers, they had no previous experience of flight-testing analysis work and they had to be trained.

Shortly thereafter I got a call from the Director, Personnel at HAL corporate office, Shri N.R. Mohanty wanting to know whether I would like to have a helicopter FTE who was having trouble getting along with his boss at the helicopter Flight Test Centre. This officer was Sqn. Ldr. Sukhi, a French trained helicopter FTE who had worked with me earlier at ASTE. He had no problems getting along with me nor I with him and I agreed to have him in the analysis team.

With this set of people from diverse backgrounds, different corporate work cultures and ill-defined lines of command and control, I had to build a flight test team to handle the most ambitious of all aeronautical projects ever undertaken in India! Aeronautics was far from my mind at that stage as I had to solve the human relationship problem first. I could very easily have insisted that everyone from HAL should work full-time with me at NFTC but I had to keep in mind Dr Kalam's advice not to rock the boat too much. I decided to motivate every one to give his best to the project regardless of organizational affiliations and delegate responsibility as much as possible. I could not possibly monitor every activity that was going on. I had to lay down priorities for myself and my first priority was to ensure safety of flight testing and this meant I had to pay particular attention to the FCS. The FCS was the most technologically advanced system on board TD-1, so I decided to get involved in its development down to the last detail.

After reviewing the status of development of the FCS and all other components and systems of TD-1, I said to myself that first flight was at least five years away. My gut feeling was that it would take place towards the end of 1999 or in the first half of 2000. Dr Kalam, Dr Kota and all the Project Directors said it would be by December 1996. I am sure this aggressive schedule was mentioned to keep Team LCA on its toes and drive the programme hard. I did not argue with them. Time would tell whose prediction was right.

I was caught on the horns of a dilemma, because IAF modernization plans would be affected by delays in the LCA programme and national security issues were involved. As the senior most IAF officer involved with the programme it was my duty to inform Air HQ about my estimate of the date of first flight. On the other hand ADA may feel that I was not being loyal to the LCA programme if I informed Air HQ about my estimate of the date of first flight which was so much at variance with their estimate. In the end my sense of duty won over and I did inform Air HQ about the expected delay.

There was no point in having a large team at NFTC because first flight was so far away. With the small team of nine personnel, the three from HAL being available only part-time,

I started attacking infrastructural problems. The first on my agenda was the second floor that had to be built over the HAL Flight Test Centre building to house the offices and telemetry centre of NFTC. Being a HAL building, the contract had to be awarded by HAL and with the labyrinthine procedures of defence PSUs, it took six months to get the plans approved, tenders sent out, negotiations carried out, and the contract awarded. By April 1995, construction began with a 12-month deadline for completion of the works including power and air conditioning.

The reason I had the NFTC premises built as the second floor at the HAL Flight Test Centre was because the mandate given to NFTC was only to carry flight testing for the 200–20 technology demonstration flights. Thereafter the responsibility was to shift to HAL. It made no sense to me to build the facility at a different location.

During my initial rounds I discovered to my horror that the designers from HAL, ADA and ADE (which was responsible for the FCS, both hardware and software) had not decided upon an instrumentation scheme to acquire parameters during the flight testing of TD-1. After an exhaustive and exhausting round of discussions we managed to arrive at a consensus about the number of parameters and the frequency with which they had to be acquired and recorded. Sudham Hanamanth and Wg. Cdr. Kunte drew up a list of the instrumentation hardware that had to be ordered from foreign vendors, and orders were placed by April 1995.

Development of a Multi Mode Radar (MMR) was to be an integral part of the LCA programme. I felt we would need a flying test bed aircraft to carry out flight tests of the radar before it was installed in a LCA airframe. To my surprise I found no one at ADA had thought of this requirement. The ideal test bed aircraft would have been a jet aircraft which could match the speeds of the LCA, but such an aircraft was not available. I knew an Avro 748 aircraft had been loaned by the IAF to the Centre for Airborne Systems (CABS) to act as a back up for the Avro fitted with a rotodome for the Airborne

Early Warning programme. I went and met the Director CABS, Dr K. Ramchand, and asked him whether he would take on this task of modifying the nose of the aircraft with a LCA radome. He readily agreed to do so. I then went to Dr Kota and told him to sanction this project as it would be impossible to complete development of the MMR without a test bed at the disposal of the radar design team. Project sanction to modify the Avro was accorded some time in 1995.

An important tool required for the development of a fly-by-wire FCS was a real time simulator (RTS). It gets its name from the fact the mathematical flight model of the aircraft developed by the designers can be run in real time on a high speed digital computer. With good visual cues provided by modern graphics engines, test pilots can actually fly it like a real aircraft, and assess its handling qualities (HQ) with a particular version of the CLAW installed in the mathematical model. HQ is the term used in aeronautics to describe the way an aircraft responded to control inputs made by the pilot while flying the aircraft.

ADE had developed a RTS but the test pilots were very unhappy with it. They did not like the visuals available in it and said it was not possible to critically assess HQ on the approach to landing, leave alone land the aircraft. They had recently flown the far superior simulator available at BAe, Warton, UK, and quite naturally compared the ADE simulator with what they had used earlier. I looked into this problem and found we needed a powerful new computer with good graphics capability to solve the problem. Silicon Graphics of the USA had just then introduced their new Infinity series of computers with the Reality Engine graphics module. It met our requirements and we decided to pay rupees five crore for this machine, to improve the RTS to a state which the test pilots would find acceptable. It took about two months of paper work and negotiations with the vendor, before we were able to place the order for the computer in October1994 with the delivery promised in July 1995.

Though my initial assessment had indicated that first flight of TD-1 was at least five years away, I knew there was no time to lose because such a lot of preparatory work was yet to be done. I listed the following Key Result Areas (KRAs):

(a) Assessment by the test pilots and flight test engineers of the HQs of each version of the CLAW as it was developed by the CLAW team, both in the yet to be developed RTS as well as the In Flight Simulation (IFS) aircraft in the USA .
(b) Ensuring the flight test team acquired profound knowledge and understanding of every aspect of the aircraft's airframe, engine, FCS, mission computer, general systems like the hydraulic system, electrical system, etc. functionality of all software driven monitoring and control systems and operating limits of all systems.
(c) Monitoring the development process of all aircraft sub-systems which were still under development.
(d) Development of the aircraft flying manual and normal, and emergency-operating procedures by closely interacting with the design team.
(e) Developing a flight test instrumentation scheme for TD-1 based on the list of parameters the design groups wanted to monitor in flight or analyse later. This required the setting up of the telemetry monitoring station, including acquisition and installation of hardware, development of necessary software to handle the data stream, communications and the format of the display screens of the monitoring consoles.
(f) Planning and executing some lead in flight test projects with the help of the ASTE to develop new flight test techniques.
(g) Involving the flight test team in the development of four important test facilities, namely, the RTS, Cockpit Evaluation Facility (CEF), Dynamic Avionics Integration Rig (DAIR) and the FCS integration rig called the Iron Bird.
(h) Monitor the progress of the development of the MMR test bed aircraft.

After I wrote out the eight KRAs, I sat back and looked at them for a long while. Now that I had it all in front of me I felt confident I would be able to deliver the goods because I knew precisely what was required to be done in each of the eight areas but for one nagging doubt. Would all the diverse groups from different agencies work together for a common goal? I dispelled the doubt by telling myself that I was the leader and it was up to me to get the job done.

CHAPTER 6

Quadruplex Digital Fly-by-Wire and the Glass Cockpit

Before the reader starts wondering what fly-by-wire technology is all about, I will explain the system in simple terms. In a conventional aircraft there is a mechanical link between the control column in the cockpit and the control surfaces. While flying the aircraft pilots move the control surfaces to the required extent based on their training, skill and experience. In a fly-by-wire aircraft there is no such direct mechanical link. When the pilot moves the control column, the movement is converted into an electrical signal which goes to a computer. The computer in turn sends another electrical signal modified by a control law, which takes into account the flight conditions of the aircraft, to move the control valve of an electro-hydraulic actuator. The control valve allows the actuator ram which is attached to the control surface, to move to an extent determined by the law.

Modern fly by-wire-systems use a high speed digital computer for this purpose and it is called the Digital Flight Control Computer (DFCC). To provide adequate safety the computer is made quadruplex, which means it has four independent processors carrying out computations at the same time. They do so in a synchronized fashion, but each of them has an independent output which is carried by its own channel. If one channel fails, the other three are adequate to perform the mission safely. If two channels fail, the FCS will be good enough to get the aircraft back on the ground. If three channels fail, it will be time to abandon the aircraft, as it will not be safe to be airborne with no back-up in case the last channel should also fail. The computer hardware is designed and built to achieve a reliability level, expressed as the probability of loss of control (PLOC) of the aircraft only once in ten million (1×10^{-7}) cycles.

In a quadruplex FCS, no mechanical or electronic back-up system is provided to operate the flight controls. In the LCA, the lack of a back-up posed an additional problem because the aircraft was designed to be unstable in the pitch axis. A bit of explanation will be required here for the lay reader. An aircraft has three axes, one running from nose to tail called the X or longitudinal axis, one from wingtip to wingtip called the Y or lateral-axis and the one perpendicular to the other two and passing through the Centre of Gravity (CG) of the aircraft called the Z or normal axis. The aircraft pitches up and down around the lateral or pitch axis, rolls to the left or right around the longitudinal or roll axis and yaws to the left or right around the normal or yaw axis. In a longitudinally stable aircraft should a disturbance make the nose pitch up, the natural stability of the configuration would make the nose pitch down to return it to the original condition of flight. In a longitudinally unstable aerodynamic configuration the nose would continue to pitch upwards unless the controls were moved artificially by the FCS to return the aircraft to its original state. Ah! the reader might say but why can't the pilot do this himself? The reason why he cannot do it, is because the aircraft would go out of control in less than a quarter of a second, whereas, normal pilot reaction which is about half a second would not allow him to take corrective action in time. Only a fly-by-wire system would be able to sense the pitching motion and move the control surface in time to prevent disaster. Why go through all this trouble of designing an unstable aircraft? It is done because an aircraft which is unstable in the pitch axis can turn very quickly, and that sort of agility is required in modern air combat situations. In addition fly-by-wire technology enables the designers to introduce 'limiters' which prevent the pilot from exceeding any of the laid-down limits of normal acceleration or 'g', angle of attack and rate of roll or bank angle. In other words technology prevents the pilot from getting into trouble by always making him fly the aircraft within cleared design limits and hence flying becomes safer. The LCA was designed to be stable about the roll and yaw axes, but the control surfaces, ailerons and rudder, are moved by the fly-by-wire system.

Our BAe consultants spent a lot of time explaining to us that adequate redundancy was provided by the quadruplex concept itself and there was no need for a back-up, as the aircraft would be on the ground well before all four channels failed. The Wright Laboratory engineers were not so forthright in their advice. They neither said it was needed nor that it was not needed. They said it was the design team's choice depending on the level of confidence reposed in the FCS. For us in India, fly-by-wire was unknown territory and our confidence was not high; but Air HQ was adamant that a back-up system was required. After much discussion at various levels it was decided to provide a digital back-up (DBU) system which would be a simplified version of the main CLAW. In hindsight, I think this decision was taken more to get on with the development of the FCS, rather than waste time trying to convince Air HQ to change its stance.

The software in the DFCC is broadly divided into two parts. The first part is the CLAW which decides how much the control surfaces should move depending on flight conditions. From a mathematical flight model of the aircraft based on wind tunnel and Computational Fluid Dynamics (CFD) data, control engineers calculate the amount of control deflection required to control the aircraft at various points in the flight envelope, and create a big look up table which is stored in the computer memory. The flight conditions are sensed by the air data probes on the aircraft and passed to the computer. The computer accesses the look up table in real time and decides the amount of control deflection required. Each computational frame lasts 12.5 milliseconds or in other words is repeated 80 times per second, but the actual movement of the control surface takes place about twice per second. The second part of the software manages the various components of the system like actuators, sensors, air data transducers and takes care of redundancy management.

The entire software running into several tens of thousands of lines of code was written in the Ada language. The software was developed at ADE with help from the MMCS engineers. They introduced the Indian team to the rigour with which flight safety critical software had to be developed. In addition to the very structured and controlled development process backed by documentation, each line of code was subjected to a very stringent verification process before being ported into the computer. To do this work ADA set-up an Independent Verification and Validation (IV&V) team under Dr K. Karunakar. He was ably assisted by two lady scientists, Shailaja Prasad and Ahalya Chandrashekar. CEMILAC, the certification agency, worked closely with this team. The IV&V team worked alongside the software development team at ADE but was independent of it. The IV&V team made a most praiseworthy contribution not only to the successful development of the fly-by-wire FCS, but also to the verification of half a million lines of software code in the aircraft. It took close to 100 man-years of effort to develop the FCS software required for the first block of flights. To reach the stage of final operational clearance (FOC) for the LCA may well require an equivalent effort. Who said fly-by-wire was easy?

A bit of explanation is required for the terms verification and validation as used in the development of software controlled systems. Verification is the process by which it is ensured that the software has been developed according to accepted industry procedures and standards. It ensures 'doing things right'. Validation is the process of checking that the software is actually delivering the functionality of the whole system that the designers are looking for. This requires hardware in the loop simulation and ensures that the system is 'doing the right things'.

CLAW development was the task in which test pilots and test engineers had to be involved from the very beginning. As mentioned earlier when I arrived at ADA the two HAL test pilots and one flight test engineer from ASTE were at the BAe simulator at Warton, UK, assessing the first version of the CLAW. The pilots were required to assess whether the HQ exhibited by a particular version of CLAW allowed them to execute a given phase of flight-like take off, approach and landing, aerobatics, weapon delivery, air combat manoeuvring or close formation with another aircraft safely, at an acceptable level of workload. The HQ exhibited in each phase was assessed on a scale of 1 to 10 with 1 standing for excellent HQ which required no further change to the CLAW and 10 indicating that a crash was inevitable! This rating scale is called the Cooper-Harper rating scale or more simply, C-H rating.

The CLAW team was located at the Flight Mechanics and Controls Division (FMCD) at the National Aerospace Laboratories (NAL), a laboratory under the Council for Scientific and Industrial Research (CSIR), at Bangalore. It was headed by Dr Srinath Kumar who was an old friend as we had worked together on two important development projects while I was at ASTE a decade earlier. He had a small team of control engineers including Dr Shyam Chetty and Dr Girish Deodhare, and simulation specialists like Padma Madhuranath working with him. They were supported by two BAe control engineers Harry Widger and Keith Hulme, who visited Bangalore periodically. The involvement of BAe specialists was covered under the consultancy agreement signed by HAL with BAe for installing the FCS in TD-I.

NAL also had a small group within the FMCD which was dedicated to parametric identification. Parametric identification is a mathematical technique by which aircraft aerodynamic and stability and control data can be derived from flight test data, obtained by applying specially tailored control inputs at various flight conditions. This group was headed by Dr Raoul. He along with Parameshwaran, Girija Gopalarathnam and other scientists had honed their skills for over a decade by carrying out joint projects with the ASTE.

When I was Commandant ASTE, I had visited Israel in

1993 to look at the Israel Aircraft Industries (IAI) proposal to upgrade the MiG-21 Bis. What struck me most forcefully during that visit was the large number of pilots-cum-engineers who were working on various projects. A young avionics engineer who was showing me the Head Up Display (HUD) to be installed in the MiG-21 told me he was an active F-16 pilot who flew regularly with his squadron over weekends! Small wonder then that Israeli engineers were able to produce equipment which was exactly what the pilots needed because they were pilots themselves!

Unfortunately that situation did not obtain in India. A vast gulf of mutual ignorance and suspicion separated pilots and engineers as neither fully understood the difficulties and demands of the other person's job. I was determined to change this situation during the development of the CLAW for TD-1.

Sqn. Ldr. B.B. Misra was a test pilot serving at ASTE when I came across him for the first time in 1991. He was a self-taught electronics and computer whiz kid who had single-handedly repaired a complex electro optical tracking system at ASTE. He had met with an unfortunate scooter accident in 1993 and had been grounded medically for six months. When I returned from Israel, I spoke to Misra and told him that he was the type of test pilot who should get into the development of airborne systems. I asked him whether he would like to be involved in the development of the LCA'S CLAW. He agreed to give it a try. I then rang up Dr Srinath Kumar and suggested he try out Misra in the CLAW team as I felt piloting inputs early in the development of the CLAW of the fly-by-wire system would be invaluable for achieving the aim of providing good HQ to the LCA. Dr Kumar was so happy with Misra that he kept him in the CLAW team for six years! Misra's contribution to CLAW development can only be described as extraordinary.

Misra and simulation specialists at the FMCD, NAL, developed a simulator which was dubbed the Engineer in Loop Simulator (ELS). Misra tested the CLAW versions as the control engineers developed them and gave instant comments on the HQ of that particular version. This way the CLAW group was able to fine tune the control laws to a very large extent even before it landed up in the RTS at ADE for evaluation by the three project test pilots. While the RTS slowly evolved to an acceptable standard there was a constant barrage of complaints from the test pilots about the unsatisfactory state of the simulator for HQ evaluation. I had no choice but to wait for the new Silicon Graphics computer that had been ordered.

As part of the assistance to be provided for the LCA project by the USAF, ADA, ADE and CLAW team engineers worked with flight control specialists from Wright Laboratories at Dayton, Ohio, USA. This laboratory had access to three In Flight Simultation (IFS) aircraft operated by a private company called Calspan at Buffalo, New York. Two of these aircraft, a T-33 trainer and an F-16 trainer, belonged to the USAF. The third, a Lear executive jet, belonged to the company. All three aircraft had their fly-by-wire flight controls extensively modified to be able to simulate the HQ of similar types of aircraft by feeding in the required data into their flight control computers. This was a very useful tool as test pilots could get to evaluate the HQ of the aircraft they were going to fly in a real world environment, especially during the take-off, approach and landing phases which were difficult to simulate realistically in the RTS.

A question often asked about IFS is 'How is it possible to simulate the HQ of a particular aircraft in a different one?' The first requirement of the simulator aircraft is that it should have a fly-by-wire FCS with a programmable computer. When a pilot flies an aircraft he makes numerous control inputs and constantly assesses the HQ of the aircraft. He bases his assessment on the initial response of the aircraft within the first one to two seconds following a control input. FCS engineers are able to 'tweak' the initial response of the simulator aircraft by modifying the software in its flight control computer, to match the initial response to control inputs of the aircraft being simulated. Steady state response would, however, be different because the aerodynamic shapes of the simulated aircraft and the simulator aircraft would be different. It must be remembered that the test pilot can carry out HQ evaluation only within the flight envelope of the simulator aircraft.

ADA very wisely decided to follow the advice of Wright Laboratories and signed a contract with Calspan to carry out IFS of the LCA CLAW in three phases. In the first, the CLAW would be tested in a very limited flight envelope in the Lear Jet in December 1994. This would be more in the nature of a confidence-building exercise for both the CLAW engineers and the test pilots about the utility of the In Flight Simulation exercise. The second phase would be in the T-33 in June 1995 and the third in the F-16 in June 1996.

I was 53 years old when I came to ADA but still medically fit to fly fighter aircraft. At that time, in my 32 years in the IAF, I had been in active flying for 29 years having managed to avoid prolonged ground postings by specializing as a test pilot and remaining medically fit all the time. I had 5150 hours in my log book on 72 different types of aircrafts. Surely this hard-earned experience would be useful in the development of the LCA's CLAW! I decided I would get fully involved in the development of the CLAW by flying the RTS as well as the IFS aircraft. Test pilots the world over are known for their strong opinions and I felt I should be in a position to arbitrate or make an informed decision in case a conflict of opinion arose between the three project test pilots.

The term Glass Cockpit refers to a modern cockpit in which all the round dialled electro-mechanical instruments have been replaced with MFDs and a HUD. The MFDs chosen for the two TD aircraft were colour Active Matrix Liquid Crystal Displays (AMLCDs). Alpha Numerics (letters of the English alphabet and numbers from 0 to 9), and other symbology in 256 colours derived from the three primary colours red, green and blue could be displayed on them. Information required by the pilot to take-off, navigate, perform his operational mission, deliver his weapons, cope with enemy threats, return to base and land is gathered by sensors on board the aircraft, processed by a mission computer and then displayed on the MFDs and HUD.

The primary sensor in the aircraft is the Inertial Navigation System (INS). This system consists of accelerometers and ring laser gyros which sense aircraft acceleration along and rotation around its body axes. The fundamental principle of inertial navigation is that the double integral of acceleration with respect to time, gives distance travelled. If the starting point is known and acceleration along the direction of flight measured, then one would know exactly where one was after a given interval of time. The INS in the TD aircraft was from Honey-well of the USA. Air data and temperature probes on the aircraft enabled the DFCC and mission computer to derive true airspeed, Mach number, and other quantities required for navigation and weapon delivery. Mach number is the ratio of true air speed of the aircraft to the speed of sound with Mach 1, indicating the speed of sound. The ratio is named after Ernst Mach, a famous German physicist.

The mission computer in the TD aircraft was based on the Intel 386 processor which would seem pedestrian compared to present-day chips. Back in 1986 it was the fastest processor available and was chosen as it was more than adequate for the purpose of technology demonstration. The mission computer hardware was developed by Ramalingam and his team at the Advanced Systems Integration and Evaluation Organization (ASIEO), which had Dr K.G. Narayanan as the Director when it was formed in 1985. The software was developed by Wg. Cdr. Vishweshwariya and his team at ADA. It took about 120 man-years of coding effort. The IV&V team vetted this software as well.

In 1988 when I was the CTP at the ASTE, Kitcha, then DASR at Air HQ had asked me to place a team of test pilots and flight test engineers at the disposal of ADE for the purpose of evolving the top level functionality requirement document for the mission computer. I chose test pilots who had flown the three most modern aircraft in the IAF inventory at that point in time, the Darin Jaguar, Mirage 2000 and Mig-29. They brought a lot of real world experience to bear on the group tasked to evolve the document. Due to this very far-sighted move, the development of the mission computer software started with a wealth of operational inputs and proceeded on the correct lines to meet user requirements when the time came to fly the Technology Demonstrators.

As far as flight testing the glass cockpit was concerned, we at NFTC had to understand the functionality of the mission computer software and ensure that all the information required by the pilot appeared at the right time at the right place. The control of the displays was with the Hands on Throttle and Stick (HOTAS) switches on the throttle and stick. All the HOTAS functions had to be evaluated in the CEF by the test pilots and accepted by them after looking at ergonomics, ease of operation and overall effect on cockpit workload. Before going to the aircraft we had to check out the display symbology at the DAIR at ADE in which the entire avionics system of the aircraft was reproduced with the actual hardware in place. By coupling it to an aircraft flight model, the DAIR could also be flown like the RTS. The NFTC pilots 'flew' the DAIR just to see whether the information required to fly the aircraft and perform the mission, appeared at the correct time and place in an intelligible form during an actual flight profile. The confidence of the pilots and their familiarity with the avionics system as an integrated whole had to be developed by doing a lot of 'flying' on the DAIR and the CEF. The development of these two ground-based rigs itself required continuous involvement of the test pilots and flight test engineers over a period of three years.

CHAPTER 7

In Flight Simulation and Roll Out of TD-1

In December 1994, Wg. Cdr. Rakesh Sharma, Sqn. Ldrs. Baldev Singh, Uday Shankar, Misra and I went to Calspan, Buffalo, New York, to attend a two-week capsule on the approach to testing fly-by-wire FCS equipped aircraft. At the end of the capsule we were to try out the CLAW in the Lear jet at one particular speed on approach, flare out for landing and actual touchdown. The theoretical knowledge we gained about test techniques for fly-by-wire aircraft was most useful. The stability and control of the aircraft was ensured by the 'controller' or the CLAW designed by the control engineers. As mentioned in the previous chapter, to decide whether the CLAW was doing its job in an acceptable manner, the test pilots and flight test engineers had to assess the HQ of the aircraft. The test pilot was the supreme arbiter of the acceptability of a CLAW and was required to have an intimate knowledge of the role of the aircraft and the environment in which the mission would be performed. This was the crucial contribution of the test pilots in the development of a fly-by-wire FCS.

The Calspan pilots and engineers we worked with were a really nice bunch of guys. We had the pleasure of interacting with test pilots Mike Parrag and Lou Knotts, and with a FCS specialist Dr K. Govindaraj who had studied at the same high school as I did in Bangalore. The CLAW team engineers, Shyam Chetty, Girish Deodhare and Misra had gone there a fortnight earlier to work with the Calspan specialists and to set-up the simulation in the Lear jet. The two evaluation pilots and I were pleasantly surprised to find we could comfortably land the Lear jet in the designated touchdown area using the LCA CLAW. More importantly the NFTC and CLAW teams developed a good working relationship with the Calspan engineers which stood us in good stead during our subsequent visits to Calspan.

On our return, the CLAW team started working at a furious pace to get the next version of the CLAW ready for RTS evaluation by the project test pilots. Wg. Cdr. Rajiv Kothiyal joined NFTC in March 1995. The Calspan engineers had told us to thoroughly evaluate the CLAW in the RTS before the next in flight simulation exercise in the T-33 scheduled for June 1995.

At this stage I must explain the working of the CLAW to the reader in simple terms. The term 'gain' means the amount of control power (control surface deflection), that is applied by the FCS at any given instant of time to modify aircraft motion around its three axes. The term 'phase' means the instant of time at which the control input is applied which could be either in phase with aircraft motion in which case it would assist the motion or it could be out of phase in which case it would oppose the motion. The whole aim of the CLAW engineers was to ensure that these phase and gain parameters were within limits prescribed by theory, to ensure control of the aircraft throughout its flight envelope.

If the gains depend upon the dynamic air pressure (speed and height of the aircraft) felt by the control surfaces, they are called scheduled gains. If they are invariant with flight condition, they are called fixed gains and they restrict the flight envelope of the aircraft quite drastically, because of the problem of having to respect gain margins. In 1995, we in our ignorance had decided to fly the aircraft with scheduled gains from its very first flight onwards, because scheduled gains implied that all the position errors in the air data system and characteristics of the transducers were known to the CLAW designers. This was not true because actual in flight calibration of errors in the system was yet to be done.

Since the CLAW was being designed with scheduled gains, we had to evaluate it in the full flight envelope of the LCA. This was a big task and required many hours of work in the RTS. As HQ assessments are based on subjective pilot opinion, each pilot had to do his own assessment and evaluate the HQ observed on the C-H scale. Frequent breakdowns of the RTS at ADE did not help matters. I flew the RTS regularly and checked out the problem areas pointed out by the project test pilots.

As HQ was being assessed subjectively by the pilots, I felt at least one more pilot's opinion would be required to draw iso-opinion plots and clearly identify problem areas. Wg. Cdr. Raghunathan Nambiar was a senior test pilot with Mirage 2000 experience available at ASTE, and with Air HQ's permission, I brought him into the evaluation team.

Without consulting the test pilots, I decided that at the next IFS session we would try out a method of reporting HQ assessments which would prevent one pilot's opinion from influencing that of another. I would allot each pilot a number with which he would identify himself in his report. In addition I would make the pilots carry out 'blind' assessments by not discussing HQ ratings with each other before writing the report. The FTE, Sqn. Ldr. Uday Shankar would then collate the reports and draw the iso-opinion plots. These plots would be discussed with the CLAW engineers later.

Since I had decided to participate in the IFS sessions for CLAW development as one of the evaluation pilots, I had to put in some flying practice. I obtained permission from Air HQ to fly at the ASTE and regularly flew various types of aircraft till I was satisfied that my flying skills were back in shape.

In June 1995 we went to Calspan again and flew the NT-33 for about three weeks at the Niagara Falls Air Force Base near Buffalo, New York. The four test pilots and I carried out 300 approaches and landings and we were very happy with the HQ provided by the CLAW in the crucial approach and landing phase. We did find a problem while banking the aircraft. The roll acceleration was too high and our helmets banged against the side of the canopy. We asked the CLAW engineers to reduce this parameter and the problem was solved. At the RTS in Bangalore, we were always asking them to do the opposite! This was only one of the many ways in which IFS helped us to 'calibrate' the HQ seen in the RTS with HQ required in the real world. The CLAW, however, was of the scheduled gain variety. The system of 'blind' assessments of HQ worked very well and we decided to use it for RTS work also. We spent some time in each sortie testing the transition logic developed by ADA engineers to smoothly go to the DBU from the main Operational Flight Programme (OFP), should any problem occur.

During a weekend all of us went to the Niagara Falls and spent a wonderful afternoon looking at the awesome sight of millions of gallons of fresh water cascading over the rocks. A cruise in a launch called *The Maid of the Mist* took us to the foot of the Horseshoe Falls and a quick trip to view the falls from the Canadian side rounded off an unforgettable experience.

On my way back to India, I stopped over at Warton, UK, to fly the BAe simulator as the HAL pilots were insistent that unless our own RTS was developed to the same standard of realism it would not be possible to evaluate the LCA CLAW especially in the approach and landing phases. When I sat in the simulator for the first time I was amazed by the visual scene before my eyes. It was very much like the real world, one saw on approach to landing at an airfield. As far as the HQ experienced in the simulator in which the mathematical model of the LCA had been loaded, I felt our RTS at Bangalore was as good and if good visuals were provided our pilots would be happy. I did, however, notice some abnormal behaviour during take off. At the moment of leaving the ground the nose of the aircraft tended to pitch up slightly before it climbed away normally. I had resolved that no anomaly however small, should be left unattended and decided to take a more detailed look at the problem back home.

During this visit to Warton I managed to mix business with a bit of pleasure. I fulfilled a long held desire to visit the St Andrews golf course near Edinburgh in Scotland by flying there during the weekend and watching a day's play at the British Open Golf Championship of that year. For any golfer this was the equivalent of a religious pilgrimage!

On my return to India, I presented the results of our IFS exercise to a packed conference room at ADA in the presence of Dr Kalam. Everyone was thrilled to hear we were making progress in understanding how to design a CLAW for a fly-by-wire FCS. Dr Kalam said we should plan to have a formal roll out of TD-1 as soon as possible as the scheduled roll out date for TD-1 of February 1995 had already slipped.

The main delay was due to slow progress in the manufacture of the first set of wings made of carbon composites. The National Wing Team headed by Dr K.N. Raju, former Director of NAL, had designed the wings, but they were being manufactured at the composite shop at HAL Aircraft Research and Design Centre (AR&DC) under the watchful eye of K.V. Sreevatsan General Manager (AR&DC). Sreevatsan was one of the senior managers at HAL who did not share the apathy shown by corporate management to the LCA programme. On the contrary, he was very committed, driving his team hard to make sure TD-1's airframe got ready in time for a roll out before the end of 1995. HAL technicians had never worked with composites before and there was a learning curve involved. HAL asked for help from BAe and a few experienced technicians came from Warton UK, and assisted the HAL workforce. The documents of the first set of wings were handed over to Sreevatsan by Dr Raju at a ceremony at NAL in June 1995 just before the NFTC team left for Calspan. The composite wings were mated to the fuselage in September 1995; quite remarkably, when the wings were pushed into place for the first time for the wing attachment bolts to be inserted, the bolts could be inserted into the bolt holes by hand. The fit was so precise! This was due to extensive use of Computer Aided Design (CAD)/Computer Aided Manufacture

(CAM) facilities and investments in jigs, fixtures and tooling. TD-1 was beginning to look like an aircraft albeit with empty innards! Electrical looms, flight test instrumentation looms, hydraulic, fuel and environmental control pipelines and a myriad other items were yet to be installed. After installation, all systems had to be checked for proper functioning. Clearly this was not possible to do in a hurry and a decision was taken to install as much of the looms, plumbing and equipment as possible and roll out the aircraft some time in November 1995. System check-outs were to be done later.

While the NFTC pilots were busy with CLAW development, Wg. Cdr. Raveendran, the other flight test engineer, was working with ASTE to carry out an experiment to develop a new technique to calibrate the air data system using the INS on board the aircraft and the Global Positioning System (GPS), to accurately determine the aircraft's position in time and space. A Jaguar fighter at ASTE was used as the test bed to develop this technique. The experiment was a success and the NFTC team gained invaluable experience and confidence to do the air data calibration on the LCA when required.

Sudham Hanamanth and Wg. Cdr. Kunte were busy getting the instrumentation looms (bundles of wires) installed in the aircraft, and accepting instrumentation hardware which had started arriving from various vendors, while Nalte and his analysis team were deeply involved in developing the software to display telemetered data on the monitoring screens.

In July 1995, as part of the contract signed by HAL with BAe for integration of the FCS on the aircraft, a flight test engineer, Terry Smith from Warton, UK, spent two weeks at NFTC. He had worked on a number of development programmes for over 25 years and had a wealth of experience to share with us. He said the flight test team should prepare a flight test plan for every major system on the aircraft and not just for the aircraft as a whole. He said once we had all the test plans written down it would be easy to slot specific test requirements into each sortie profile when flight testing actually started. When we did that, we found we had to prepare

27 documents covering all the systems on the aircraft! He wanted us to send him these documents to him for his comments by the end of the year. He went on to say that for the first block of flights the aircraft should have an independent set of pressure instruments like the air speed indicator, altimeter, angle of attack and vertical speed indicators. It was the practice at BAe not to rely solely on air data which had been processed by the mission computer, until the air data system itself had been calibrated during flight testing. All that he said made eminent sense to me and I told the pilots and engineers at NFTC to start acting on all the points he had raised. It was a most useful visit.

As part of the management, I had to attend endless meetings on the status of a large number of items being developed indigenously. In addition, there was a core Programme Co-ordination Team (PCT) of which I was a member. The PCT met every Monday at 5 p.m. These meetings usually ended past 7 p.m. and I attended 320 PCT meetings before we flew TD-1! Whew! Fighter aircraft sure are difficult to design and fly!

On 19 November 1995, Prime Minister P.V. Narasimha Rao pressed a button to raise a curtain to reveal LCA TD-1 to a large gathering of dignitaries at the prototype hangar at HAL BC. The Prime Minister exhorted everyone to ensure that the aircraft entered IAF service by 2003. He made a particular mention of the need to develop our own engine to power the aircraft, to avoid being held to ransom by engine manufacturers of the developed world. I could see Frank Wisner, the US ambassador, squirming in his seat! Chairman R.N. Sharma hogged the limelight and Dr Kota who was stricken with laryngitis could be barely heard when he spoke. Dr Kalam told the audience that the aircraft would fly by November 1996. ACM Kaul who was to demit office at the end of 1995, sounded a note of caution when he said the LCA project could be considered a success only when the aircraft flew in IAF colours, every day, in far corners of our vast country.

After the roll out ceremony there was a tea party. ACM

Kaul took me to Dr Kalam and in my presence he said, 'This chap is likely to be promoted shortly and unless you make necessary arrangements to retain him by creating a suitable vacancy, I will be forced to end his deputation to ADA'. Dr Kalam said he would do the needful. This was the first inkling I had that I was going to be promoted to the rank of Air Marshal.

ACM S.K. Sareen became the CAS on 1 January 1996. He visited ADA in February that year and I told him the aircraft could not possibly fly during his tenure of three years. He visited ADA again in August 1998 just a few months before he was due to retire.

One of the limitations of IFS is that the flight envelope in which the 'simulated' aircraft can be evaluated is restricted to only a portion of the 'simulator' aircraft's envelope. The F-16 trainer in which we were to try out the CLAW in June 1996 had a bigger envelope than the T-33 we had flown the previous year. We had to do a lot of flying in the RTS to check out the new version of the CLAW developed by our control engineers, and I was handicapped by the fact that Wg. Cdr. Nambiar had left the team to finish his command tenure in a fighter squadron.

The new computer for the RTS arrived towards the middle of 1995, and I thought the RTS would improve both in realism and reliability. Unfortunately, that did not happen. The visual scene was still not very good and simulator freezes were occurring with alarming regularity. I requested the ADA simulation engineers to improve the wiring by bringing it up to engineering standards as I did not know why the RTS was so failure prone. Whenever the simulator's visuals froze, an engineer would run to the computer and tap a few keys and the simulator would spring back to life. This did nothing to enhance the confidence of the evaluation pilots as they did not feel they were testing the real 'LCA'. In spite of the unsatisfactory state of the RTS I insisted the CLAW be evaluated by the three pilots before we went back to Calspan.

I now had to get to the bottom of the anomaly I had noticed

during the visit to the BAe simulator in the UK. I discussed the problem with the test pilots and the CLAW team. Dr Srinath Kumar was of the view that it could be a problem associated with the mathematical model of the undercarriage which may not be mirroring reality correctly. Further investigation revealed that the three simulation groups at HAL, NAL and ADE had independently developed their models from the same set of data and said there was no need to put the same model everywhere. I disagreed and said I wanted the model developed by the CLAW team to be thoroughly verified and installed in the RTS at ADE. The test pilots then identified the problem in a more critical fashion, and the CLAW team modified the CLAW to solve it. I was still not happy. Making use of our consultancy agreement with BAe, I asked them to send one of their experienced test pilots to comment on the HQ at take-off. Later that year Paul Hopkins, came down and evaluated the LCA's take-off characteristics in the RTS. I was very impressed with the way he went about his work. He got into the RTS one morning and said he would like to be left alone for three hours. He did a very large number of take-offs and said the HQ on take-off was quite acceptable. He did make one comment the significance of which I did not appreciate at that moment. During discussions, he said the flight envelope we had indicated to him was extremely generous for an aircraft which had not been flown yet. This was because we had shown him the scheduled gain envelope! To my specific query about the state of the RTS especially the visuals, he said it was quite satisfactory and adequate for the task of HQ evaluation. I hoped one day the NFTC pilots would say the same!

The CLAW engineers had modified the software by absorbing the lessons learned during the T-33 evaluation, but it was still a scheduled gain CLAW. We evaluated it extensively and got ready for the visit to Calspan in time. The F-16 trainer we were to fly was called VISTA (Variable in Flight Simulation Trainer Aircraft).

In June 1996, Rakesh Sharma, Kothiyal, Baldev Singh and

Plate 1: The author on commissioning, 10 November 1962.

Plate 2: LCA TD-1 getting airborne on its first flight on 4 January 2001 at Bangalore.

Plate 3: Wg. Cdr. Rajiv Kothiyal climbing out of the cockpit of the LCA TD-1 after the historic first flight on 4 January 2001. Note the tricolour being held aloft in the background.

Plate 4: The author being congratulated by the Defence Minister, Shri George Fernandes, after the first flight of TD-1. Seen in the background is ACM A.Y. Tipnis and at the edge of the picture is Dr. V.K. Aatre DG, ADA.

Plate 5: Group photograph in front of TD-1 after first flight. Standing front row L to R—Mr. Beharilal, MD HAL (BC), Dr. C.G.K. Nair, Chairman HAL, the author, Dr. V.K. Aatre SA to RM and DG ADA, Shri George Fernandes, RM, Wg. Cdr. Rajiv Kohtiyal, ACM A.Y. Tipnis, CAS, Dr. Kota Harinarayana, Programme Director, LCA and Mr. Subir Dutta, Secy. Def. Production and Supplies, MOD.

Plate 6: Wg. Cdr. Rajiv Kothiyal at the SETP Awards ceremony at the Beverley Hilton Hotel, Los Angeles, USA on 27 September 2001. On his right is Iven C. Kinchloe IV and on his left is President of SETP for 2001, M. Lynn Hanks.

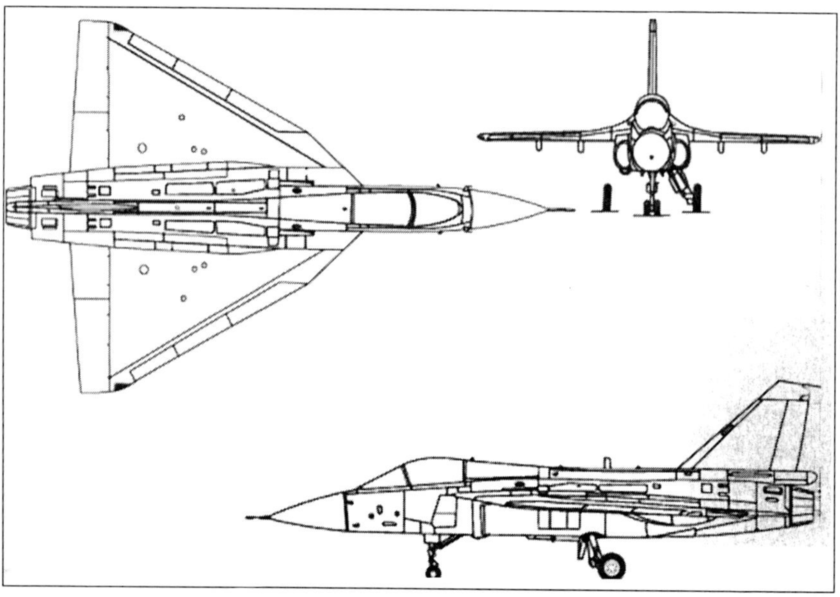

Plate 7: 3-View drawing of LCA TD-1.

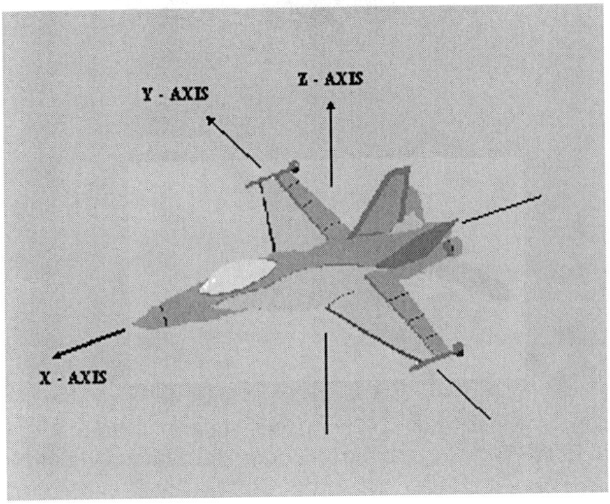

Plate 8: Three Axes of an aircraft.

Plate 9: First Flight of TD-2 on 6 June 2002.

Plate 10: NFTC personnel in early 1995.
Standing L to R—Wg. Cdr. P.K Raveendran, the author, Gautamski Vohra, Wg. Cdr. Rajiv Kothiyal, Sqn. Ldr. Uday Shankar, Wg. Cdr. Sudhakar Kunte.

Plate 11: CLAW evaluation on the T-33A at the Niagara Falls Air Force Base in the USA in June 1995. The T-33A is seen in the background.
Standing L to R—Wg. Cdr. Rajiv Kothiyal, the author, Wg. Cdr. (Retd) Rakesh Sharma, Dr Sitaram Raju (ADA), Dr K. Govindaraj (Calspan).
Kneeling in front row L to R—Wg. Cdr. Raghunathan Nambiar, Dr Shyam Chetty, CLAW engineer, Sqn. Ldr. Uday Shankar.

Plate 12: CLAW evaluation on the F-16 VISTA at Buffalo, NY, USA in July 1996. The author on the right is seen with Calspan test pilot John Ball.

Plate 13: T-33 and F-16 VISTA in formation in July 1996. The author was in the front cockpit of the T-33A with Lou Knotts of Calspan in the rear cockpit. Wg. Cdr. (Retd) Rakesh Sharma was in the front cockpit of the F-16 VISTA with John Ball of Calspan in the rear cockpit.

Plate 14: Group photograph with Dr. V.K. Aatre at Aero India, 2003.
Standing L to R—Sqn. Ldr. Thomas, Wg. Cdr. P.K. Raveendran, the author, Dr V.K. Aatre, Mr M.B. Verma, Gp. Capt. R Bhaduria, Sqn. Ldr. M.K.R. Prasad.
Kneeling L to R—Wg. Cdr. Vikram Singh and Sqn. Ldr. Sunit Krishna.

Plate 15: Formation take-off of LCA TD-1 and TD-2 in the presence of Prime Minister A.B. Vajpayee on 4 May 2003.

Plate 16: The author being greeted by Defence Minister Shri George Fernandes after the naming ceremony on 4 May 2003.
On my left are M.B. Verma, Programme Director LCA, Ashok Baweja, MD (D&D) HAL, Yogesh Kumar, Exec. Director (D&D) HAL and Air Cmde Parvez Khokar, PDFT, ADA.

Plate 17: Group photograph with the Prime Minister Atal Behari Vajpayee after the naming ceremony on 4 May 2003.
Standing L to R—Ashok Baweja, the author, Yogesh Kumar, Wg. Cdr. Raveendran, Air Cmde Khokar, the Prime Minister, Defence Minister Shri George Fernandes, M.B. Verma, Dr. V.K. Aatre, ACM S. Krishnaswamy CAS.
Kneeling L to R—Sqn. Ldr. M.K.R. Prasad, Gp. Capt. R. Bhaduria, Wg. Cdr. Vikram Singh and Sqn. Ldr. Sunit Krishna and two unidentified HAL personnel.

Plate 18: Presenting a photograph of the two Tejas aircrafts flying in formation to President Abdul Kalam at Rashtrapati Bhavan on 25 August 2003. Dr C.G.K. Nair, former Chairman HAL, is on the right.

Plate 19: No. 1 Squadron pilots at Adampur after the September 1965 Indo-Pak war. The author is standing at the extreme right.

Plate 20: MIG-23 evaluation in the Soviet Union in April 1979. The author is seen talking to Air Marshal L.M. Katre (later CAS) and Air Cmde S.K. Mehra (later CAS) after his first flight on the MIG-23 UB. The photograph was taken at the Lugovaya air base in Kazakhstan.

Plate 21: The author when he was Chief Test Pilot at ASTE in 1986. This photograph was taken during the evaluation of the Hawk AJT in the UK.

Plate 22: The author being greeted by Air Cmde. A.K. Nagalia, Commandant ASTE after his 3261st flight on the MIG-21 on 8 August 2001, his 60th birthday. In the background is Gp. Capt. Sukumar CTP, ASTE.

Plate 23: Visit to the General Electric jet engine plant at Lynn, Massachusetts, USA, in July 2002.
Standing L to R—B.D. Singh, Financial Advisor to DG ADA, Dr. K.V.L. Rao, PD Propulsion ADA, Checker, DRDO Representative in the USA, the author. Nagui Zakak and Jerry Chu of General Electric are seen on the author's left.

Plate 24: Tejas being demonstrated at Aero India 2005.

Plate 25: Tejas seen in IAF grey colour scheme with drop tanks, bombs and CCM.

Plate 26: PV-2 takes off on its first flight on 1 December 2005.

Plate 27: PV-2 on its first flight on 1 December 2005.

Plate 28: MMR test bed AVRO in flight September 1997. The Rotodome mounting pylons for the AEW programme can also be seen in the photograph.

Plate 29: The author with Sheila (left) and Nilima (centre) in December 1998.

Plate 30: The author on retirement from the IAF on 31 August 2001.

I went to Calspan. Uday Shankar came along as the FTE and we were preceded by Dr Shyam Chetty, Dr Deodhare and B.B. Misra of the CLAW team. They had gone a fortnight earlier to introduce the LCA CLAW into the VISTA's DFCC. This time the pilots we flew with were Jeff Peer, Russ Easter and John Ball, all extremely nice guys and thorough professionals. We flew the aircraft first as an F-16, before trying out the LCA in it. The basic F-16 CLAW had been designed in the late-1960s and was not very pleasant to fly especially during approach and landing. On the other hand the LCA CLAW worked very well, and I found it easier to land the F-16 with our CLAW than with the original version! We also flew a number of missions with the F-16 in close formation with the Lear jet as well as the T-33. In one historic photo opportunity we flew the F-16 and the T-33 in formation for the last time, as the T-33 was being retired and donated to the USAF museum at Dayton, Ohio, after our visit. Jeff Peer took up a photographer in his private Pitts Special while I flew the T-33 with Lou Knotts and Rakesh Sharma flew the VISTA with John Ball. This particular photograph has found its way into aviation journals and historical records. I have no doubt in my mind that the in flight simulation exercises we did at Calspan benefited us immensely for two reasons. Firstly we developed confidence in the LCA's CLAW and secondly by interacting with the Calspan pilots we learnt how fly-by-wire systems were to be tested. An equally important and perhaps more lasting benefit, was the close rapport that developed between the CLAW engineers and the test pilots and flight test engineers.

Dr Kota and Dr Prahalad came to Calspan towards the end of the exercise and the three of us along with the air-worthiness boss Nagaraj went to the Wright Laboratories at Dayton, to meet Jim Ramage, head of the Flight Controls Division, and his team of FCS specialists. I presented the results of our LCA CLAW evaluation to this team and said the F-16 was easier to land with our CLAW. When I repeated it for the second time in my presentation, Jim cut me short saying, 'It's alright General, we got the message'!

After our return to India some changes in Team LCA took place. Dr Prahlad left ADA to become Director, NAL. Dr T.G. Pai, another aerodynamicist took over as PD (TD). Sqn. Ldr. Sukhi and Wg. Cdr. Kunte left NFTC for jobs in the private sector.

On 17 September 1996 I was promoted to the rank of Air Marshal. ACM Sareen rang me up, congratulated me and asked me to stay on at ADA at least for one more year, till he did some more 'homework' regarding the positioning of Air Marshals in various appointments. I had just under three years to attain the age of superannuation and knowing the merry-go-round that goes on at the top, I agreed to stay on. I went with a new set of rank badges to Headquarters Training Command at Hebbal and requested the Air Officer Commanding-in-Chief (AOC-in-C) Air Marshal K.B. Singh, who was my senior in service, to put them on my uniform shirt. When I came out after the very brief ceremony I found three stars on the star plate of my staff car and even the flag on the bonnet had them. It finally hit me! I had reached the 'lofty' height of a three star rank after almost 34 years of service!

At work, the programme was beginning to pay the price for the hasty roll out we had done the previous year. TD-1 had to be taken apart and rebuilt with the looming and plumbing in place. One HAL supervisor at the prototype hangar said 'Sir, in my humble opinion it will take 18 months to complete this work and get the aircraft ready to do a ground run of the engine'. These proved to be prophetic words as this was said in August 1996 and we ran the F404 engine for the first time on TD-1 in April 1998!

FCS development proved to be a very complex, multi-disciplinary activity involving a host of disciplines such as the CLAW, aerodynamics, simulation, flight test, hydraulics, electrics, avionics, electronics hardware, software, actuators and development of integration rigs like the mini-bird and the Iron Bird. The final requirement was that everything had to work satisfactorily on the actual aircraft. A number of agencies were involved and there was an urgent need to bring some managerial focus on the gamut of activities going on at various work centres. In addition there were contractual issues and milestone-based payments which needed to be made to our foreign partners.

At ADE the man in charge of FCS development, was Vice Admiral S.K. Ray, popularly called 'Sting'. Sting Ray had a Masters Degree in control engineering from the Cranfield Institute of Technology, UK, and had profound knowledge of every aspect of the FCS. Ray was a good friend of mine from earlier times, and I spent long hours with him learning all the intricacies of the FCS. It will be fair to say my knowledge and understanding of the FCS was largely due to my interactions with him.

Towards the end of 1996, Dr Kalam constituted a FCS review committee to monitor progress of FCS development. Dr K.G. Narayanan, Director ADE, was appointed Chairman and had Dr Kota, Vice Admiral S.K. Ray, the Financial Adviser to DG ADA, Dr Srinath Kumar of the CLAW group, Dr Subba Reddy of the HAL Iron Bird team, and Dr Ramsheshan of CEMILAC as the main members. I insisted that there should be a flight test representative and forced my way in! There were a number of scientists at the working level who were also to attend these meetings. The charter of this committee was to review the progress of development on a bi-weekly basis and take immediate steps to remove both technical and administrative bottlenecks as they arose. We decided to meet every other Wednesday afternoon at 1430 hours, and over 100 meetings were held before the first flight of LCA TD-1.

In January 1997, I went to the Central Scientific Instrumentation Organization (CSIO) at Chandigarh. This was the laboratory under the CSIR which had been given the task of developing an indigenous HUD. I was very heartened to see the progress they had made and recommended that we should import only the bare minimum number of HUDs from a foreign supplier to meet the requirements of TD-1. I felt it would be possible to get the indigenous HUD ready in time for TD-2.

FCS development work with MMCS later acquired by

Lockheed Martin (LM) was proceeding very slowly. The CLAW code which the test pilots had accepted as satisfactory in the RTS was in the FORTRAN language, and had to be rewritten in the Ada language before it could be put in the DFCC. In addition, the DFCC hardware and additional modules of software were being developed with frequent consultations with LM who were going very slow on their advice on how to do the hardware and software integration. A number of contractual issues cropped up, and a lot of arguments went on between ADE and LM. I began to despair wondering whether I would ever see the FCS in a ready-to-fly state, as in spite of our bi-weekly review meetings there was not enough progress in DFCC hardware software integration during 1997.

In 1997, some developments took place which had far-reaching consequences on FCS development and made first flight seem an attainable goal. Our BAe consultants Harry Widger and Keith Hulme, were steadfast in their opinion that there was no need for a back-up system for the FCS. They told us not to waste any more time on an unnecessary complication. In June 1997, Dr Kota invited a team from the Defence Evaluation and Research Agency (DERA), UK to visit ADA and advise us on how to go about clearing the FCS and the aircraft for flight. We wanted to have a consultancy agreement with them. The boss of DERA was Dr Gerry Shanks and he came down with a team of six specialists and spent a week assessing the work done up to that stage by ADA and other agencies. The DERA specialists were absolutely clear in their minds about two points, (a) there was no need for a DBU (b) the first block of flights should be flown with the CLAW in the fixed gains mode. This was invaluable advice as I had long been proposing the same course of action, but Dr Kota was hesitant to follow my advice for fear of antagonizing Air HQ. Harry Widger came on a visit to the CLAW team in September 1997 and fully agreed with DERA's recommendations. He said the final clearance of the CLAW to fly could be done by the certification agency only after extensive flying by the test pilots on the RTS, which would be followed by tests on the Iron

Bird hardware in loop test rig. He said when the time came to check the functioning of the DBU on the Iron Bird, we would end up testing forever, because it was impossible to predict when a failure in the main software would occur and transition to the DBU would take place. When asked whether we would have to repeat the areas already tested with the scheduled gain CLAW he replied in the affirmative. This advice if accepted would put the clock back for us by about 9 months. I had to get the pilots to start a fresh round of RTS evaluations. I was already having enormous problems getting the two HAL pilots to go to ADE to fly the RTS on a regular basis. They were busy with production test flying duties at HAL and it was not possible for them to do justice to the LCA project as well.

The first problem to be overcome, however, was to get Dr Kalam, DG ADA, to agree to this change of tack, i.e. flying with fixed gains in the FCS without a back-up control system. Here the extreme stubbornness shown by Dr Srinath Kumar, the head of the CLAW team, saved the day. He flatly refused to have anything to do with DBU development and insisted we drop the idea of flying with scheduled gains. Dr Kota asked me for my views on what Air HQ's reaction would be. I said the new DCAS, AM Naqvi, would support any decision taken by the design team and we should not worry about any adverse reaction from the Air Force. I based my views on the fact that there was no one at senior levels who fully understood the intricacies of a fly-by-wire system. As designers we should boldly follow the advice of DERA and Harry Widger. By the time the final go ahead was given by Dr Kalam it was March 1998. All contractual problems with LM had been sorted out and DFCC development again began to move ahead at full speed.

The MMR test bed aircraft Avro 748 H-2176 with a LCA radome fitted in its nose flew for the first time in September 1997. ASTE then conducted a short flight test programme to establish the new pressure error correction (PEC) for the altimeter and the air speed indicator with the radome installed, and to check out the structural integrity of the modification. Without this test bed aircraft the development team would have had to rely on the LCA airframe for flight trials and this would have been both time consuming and expensive. Here again early identification of a potential problem allowed a solution to be found before the problem actually arose.

CHAPTER 8

Engine Ground Run, Pokharan Blasts, US Sanctions and RTS Problems

Of the 11 GE F404 F2J3 engines which were procured way back in 1988, only one was fully instrumented. The very first time I met Mr Gopalan, the Project Director (Propulsion), in 1994, I said we would need at least two instrumented engines to go through the technology demonstration phase of flight testing. Having entrusted my life to jet engines for 30 years I was fully aware of the fairly frequent requirement to down engines due to foreign objects or small bird ingestion. I requested him to initiate action to have at least two instrumented engines available before we ran the engine on TD-1's airframe for the first time. Otherwise the flight test programme was likely to get stalled every time there was a problem with the engine. Due to the long time taken for FCS development this problem was resolved and when it was time to install the engine in the airframe, we did have two instrumented engines tested and ready.

GE positioned a field service engineer, Rich Owens, at Bangalore in 1995 to help ADA engineers maintain the 11 engines. Even when not in use, jet engines have to be maintained according to a strict schedule laid down by the manufacturer.

A team of experts from GE came to ADA in October 1997 and spent a week reviewing our readiness to integrate the engine with the airframe. The GE team leader was Nagui Zakak, a Lebanese Christian, who had immigrated to the USA in the 1960s, and was now a US citizen. He was very pro-

LCA and did his best to help us in every way possible. The other members of the team were a greatly experienced lot having been involved in many different development programmes in which the GE F404 engine had been used. At the end of their visit they said we were ready to integrate the engine with the airframe.

The telemetry centre building was finally handed over to NFTC in late-1996, and I had to ensure that the telemetry system was ready for use. Fortunately for me, Sudham Hanamanth of HAL was a really good instrumentation engineer and he did a great job of integrating all the equipment sourced from various vendors into a reliable functional system. The monitoring screens and software were in place thanks to Nalte and his team, and we were in a position to monitor the functioning of all on-board systems except the FCS, which had not been installed. Flight test instrumentation on board the aircraft was a complex system with over 1200 parameters being acquired in real time and recorded on a tape recorder for subsequent analysis. Of the 1200 parameters, 400 were telemetered down for real time monitoring by the test director and the design team. Though Sudam and his men had done the calibration of all the sensors and checked out the data acquisition system the first time we would really know whether the whole system worked properly with the aircraft power system was when we ran the engine.

Mr Gopalan had retired and the new PD (Propulsion) was Dr K.V.L. Rao who was a jet engine expert and a real workaholic. He had spent many hours preparing the engines for installation on the airframe by ground running them at the test bed at the Gas Turbine Research Establishment (GTRE) and checking out the secondary power system (SPS).

The SPS consisted of an Aircraft Mounted Auxiliary Gearbox (AMAGB) developed by the Combat Vehicle Research and Development Establishment (CVRDE) at Avadi, near Chennai. The CVRDE engineers were used to designing gear boxes for battle tanks which weighed about two tons, while ADA had tasked them to design the AMAGB whose design weight budget was only 40 kg! This challenging project was readily accepted by CVRDE and the end result was a mechanical engineering marvel which weighed only 39 kg, well inside the given weight budget. The AMAGB was driven by a power take-off (PTO) shaft from the main jet engine and drove an alternator and two hydraulic pumps for the aircraft systems. A small gas turbine called the jet fuel starter (JFS) spun the main engine up to ignition rpm during start up by transferring power through the AMAGB.

The flight test team had to evolve GE F404 operating procedures and emergency actions. I had insisted that the test pilots and flight test engineers sit with the designers of each system on the aircraft and evolve both operating and emergency procedures. I knew the designers by themselves would never be able to do this because they were not aware of the requirements of the test pilots flying the aircraft. The jointly developed draft operating and emergency procedures were sent to the certification authorities for their perusal before being formally issued to the pilots as an approved checklist.

One of the problems I continuously faced at ADA and HAL, was that while the designers were very knowledgeable about their individual systems very few of them had any idea of how all systems functioned as an integrated whole on the aircraft. Only we at the NFTC had that crucial overview which was so important to test the aircraft as a single entity. A case in point was finding properly qualified and trained personnel to carry out the forthcoming engine ground run (EGR). To safely carry out a ground run the avionics of the aircraft had to be initialized which meant the person carrying out the EGR had to know all about the avionics system on the aircraft, have a good idea of the functionality of all on board systems such as hydraulics, electrics, environmental control, etc. be aware of the engine operating procedures, limitations, warnings and emergencies. There was no one at HAL or ADA who fitted the bill. I therefore decided that the persons best suited to carry out the EGR's would be the test pilots themselves. Safety was the overriding consideration.

The pilots had to practise their procedures at the CEF which was a cockpit procedure simulator developed by ADA engineers. Back in 1996 I had complained to Dr Kota about the poor state of readiness of the CEF for NFTC pilots to use to evolve procedures. He asked me to head a committee to look into the problem. When I had a look I found the problem was due to haphazard development of the facility over time. There was no proper documentation, software was not under configuration control and the wiring was in an appalling mess. I told the CEF team to adopt a 'vacuum cleaner' approach to solve the problem. This meant clearing out the room completely and starting from a top level Functionality Requirement Document (FRD), working down to hardware and software specifications and then building the facility. I also said I wanted to see engineering standard cabling in place. It took a year of arduous toil by both the NFTC team and the simulation engineers to get the CEF to simulate the functionality of all cockpit switches, controls and indications with adequate fidelity. By introducing software models of all avionics Line Replaceable Units (LRU) and integrating the flight model, it was possible to 'fly' a profile in the CEF from start up to take-off, general flying, landing and switch off. Due to early identification of the problem, when the time came for the pilots to practise their engine start up procedures and emergencies, the CEF was available.

By the end of March 1998 we were ready to commence the first phase of ground runs on TD-1. On the day of the first run Dr Kalam came down from Delhi and there was palpable excitement in the air. A cheer went up from the crowd of HAL and ADA personnel when Wg. Cdr. Rakesh Sharma entered the cockpit. At the very last moment Dr K.V.L. Rao came up to me and said there was an anomaly in the aircraft fire-warning system. In spite of the presence of Dr Kalam and the eager crowd, I called off the test for the day and said the fire-warning circuit problem had to be resolved before we could move forward. After all safety was my primary responsibility! A few days later when the problem of the fire-warning circuit was resolved Rakesh Sharma pressed the starter button for the first time and nothing happened! There was great disappointment all round but I went around telling everyone that this sort of problem was not uncommon during development and one should not get disheartened by such glitches. On 7 April 1998 the engine fired to life, but high vibration levels were noticed on the monitoring screen at the telemetry station and the Test Director Raveendran ordered a shutdown. This problem turned out to be linked to flight test instrumentation and was quickly resolved. Finally on the third attempt, we were able to carry out a proper ground run.

We completed eight ground runs and checked out the flight test instrumentation on board the aircraft as well as the telemetry system. Numerous calibration errors surfaced and the instrumentation team had to spend many hours resolving every one of them. Other on-board systems like the hydraulics, electrics, fuel, environmental control, engine bay cooling and avionics were also checked out and a host of problems were uncovered. One problem which upset me a lot was the JFS, indigenously developed by the Engine Design Bureau of HAL, which emitted clouds of white smoke every time it was started. I felt this was unacceptable for routine service use, and asked Dr K.V.L. Rao to initiate action for changes necessary to make the JFS Euro II compliant! The engineers had to resolve all problems noticed before the next phase of EGRs.

Team LCA was beginning to feel that if we could really speed up development of the FCS we could perhaps fly the aircraft before the end of 1999. Unfortunately fate had other plans. On 12 May 1998 India conducted nuclear tests at Pokharan and the very next day the US government imposed crippling economic and technology sanctions. One of the projects to be affected the most by this unforeseen development was the LCA project. Our FCS engineers working with Lockheed Martin at Binghampton NY USA were unceremoniously sent home. An Engineering Test Station (ETS) designed and developed by ADE engineers and shipped to Lockheed Martin for hardware-software integration testing of the DFCC was impounded by the US authorities. The GE engineer, Rich Owens, left Bangalore overnight and we were left high and dry. We could not approach any US company to service or repair any item sourced from them and TD-1 had a fair number on board! Difficult days were indeed upon us!

Dr Kota, all PDs and I quickly reviewed the status of development of all systems, especially the all important FCS and came to the conclusion that we were in a position to go ahead and complete at least a portion of the technology demonstration programme. Dr Kota obtained a sanction of Rs 100 crore from project funds to pursue indigenization of some crucial aircraft sub-systems. These programmes were launched without much fanfare and when completed, will increase our self-reliance in critical technologies.

I was getting very worried about the fate of FCS development. ADE engineers were in the habit of having weekly teleconferences with their counterparts at Binghampton and frequent visits to each others facilities were the order of the day. Now that sanctions had been imposed no interaction between the teams was possible, and I feared the worst. I could not have been more wrong in my assessment because the pace of FCS development actually picked up. Adversity had proved to be a terrific tonic!

As a decision had been taken to fly the first block of flights with fixed gains, the new CLAW had to be evaluated for HQ in the RTS and rewritten in the Ada language before being ported on the DFCC. The test pilots had a lot of RTS flying to do in a short time, because without their acceptance of the HQ provided by the fixed gain CLAW we could not proceed with software development. The reluctance of two out of the three test pilots at NFTC to do extensive flying on the RTS at ADE because of what was in their opinion poor visuals and frequent failures of the system, was proving to be a big stumbling block. I had to act decisively on two fronts, the pilots and the RTS.

I had made up my mind that all pilots doing prototype flying in the LCA programme should be less than 50 years of age. I had discussed this point with my friends at British Aerospace, UK, Dassault Aviation, France and Northrop Grumman, USA. All of them said prototype flying was best left to pilots in their late thirties to mid-forties. After US sanctions were applied I knew there was no chance of flying TD-1 before the end of 2000. Wg. Cdr. Rakesh Sharma would be over 50 years old by then and he was also weighed down by his other responsibilities as the CTP of HAL (BC). I spoke to him about the problem of his age and my conviction that a younger man who could focus his undivided attention on the project should be the one to pilot TD-1 on its first flight. He saw my point of view and agreed to concentrate on his CTP duties. Sqn. Ldr. Baldev Singh returned to HAL at the end of his two-year deputation to NFTC. I was left only with Wg. Cdr. Rajiv Kothiyal to fly the RTS. I went to Air HQ and asked for Wg. Cdr. Raghunathan Nambiar to be sent to ADA on deputation as soon as he had finished his squadron commander's tenure. I also asked Air HQ to show me the records of some more test pilots and I picked Sqn. Ldr. Tarun Banerjee as the third project test pilot.

Sqn. Ldr. Uday Shankar sought premature retirement from the IAF after spending five years in the programme. He had drawn up the flight test schedules for each sortie of IFS and RTS HQ evaluation and maintained an accurate record of pilot comments and the C-H ratings for each aspect of the evaluation. Without meticulous maintenance of records, it would have been impossible to draw iso-opinion plots of C-H ratings which was the basis for the acceptability or otherwise of a particular version of the CLAW. There was no doubt in my mind that he had made a valuable contribution.

I selected an experienced flight test engineer, Sqn. Ldr. M.K.R. Prasad, to join NFTC. The two new test pilots and the flight test engineer reported for duty only in August 1999. From July 1998 till August 1999, only Rajiv Kothiyal and I flew the RTS for CLAW assessment and did all the work related to pilot vehicle interface problems. Raveendran had soldiered on alone, looking at all flight test engineering issues.

The roll out of the second Technology Demonstrator (TD-2) took place on 14 August 1998. The planned schedule for technology demonstration called for the second aircraft to fly nine months after the first flight of TD-1, whenever that took place. To see the second aircraft in the hangar was a big shot in the arm for all those working on TD-1

Around this time ADA found that it had spent Rs 200 crore less than the budgeted figure for that stage of the programme. It was, therefore, decided at one of the management meetings chaired by Dr Kalam, that the money would be spent on building airframes of the first two prototypes PV-1 and PV-2 within the Phase-1 budget itself. Everyone knew the sanction for the Phase-2 budget would be given only after the successful completion of at least a 100 flights of the technology demonstration programme. Any delay in ordering the manufacture of the prototype airframes would have had a serious effect on the already much delayed entry of the LCA into service.

I told Rajiv Kothiyal to do a thorough evaluation of the problems encountered in the RTS and submit a report. I involved personnel from CEMILAC in this exercise, and when the report was ready I wrote a covering letter and sent it to Dr Kalam, who in turn sent it to Dr K.G. Narayanan (KGN), Director ADE. A few days later I got a call from KGN asking me to meet him in his office at ADE. I went across and had a frank discussion on the problems we were facing at the RTS. I said I was interested in getting the RTS to behave in a predictable and reliable manner so that HQ evaluations of the fixed gain CLAW could be completed quickly. I suggested that he should speak to his simulation engineers and ask for their views on the observations and recommendations made in the report. When KGN spoke to his engineers they endorsed everything we had said in our report! CEMILAC's advice was sought and amongst other measures, all software was brought under configuration control. This meant no software changes could be made by anyone without proper documentation which would provide traceability. After this was done, the RTS behaved in a most reliable manner and we were able to commence serious work on assessing the fixed gain CLAW's suitability for first flight.

We had to first of all define the flight envelope for first flight. I had explained earlier that the envelope would be fairly restricted with fixed gains because of the need to respect gain margins. We wanted to find out how the aircraft behaved when we went past the speed limit worked out by the CLAW group, based on theory. When the aircraft went beyond the theoretical limit by about 50 kmph, the aircraft would start pitching up and down with gradually increasing severity till it went out of control. We identified these speeds at various heights both with undercarriage UP and DOWN and after allowing for a safe margin defined the first flight envelope. We then evaluated the HQ in various phases of flight and satisfied ourselves that it was satisfactory. Next we looked at all possible FCS emergencies and evolved procedures to cope with environmental conditions like turbulence and crosswind while landing when the FCS performance had been degraded by a failure of the rudder actuator, or a pair of elevon actuators. Kothiyal and I jointly did all this work. Extensive use of the RTS contributed immensely to flight safety.

There still was a problem of interaction between HAL flight control specialists and ADE engineers. They tended to work in compartments and I knew this situation could not be allowed to continue for long. We were nearing the stage of development when the DFCC and the software had to be tested in an integrated fashion on the Iron Bird at HAL Aircraft Research and Design Centre (AR&DC). I went to Air HQ to explain my predicament to the Vice Chief of the Air Staff (VCAS) AM Tipnis who was slated to take over as the next CAS. He took me to the CAS, ACM Sareen, and I said there was a dire need to bring all FCS development under one boss, as the sort of compartmentalized development that was going on would prove disastrous when it came to flying TD-1. ACM Sareen listened to me and promised to do the needful. I invited him to review progress of the project which he had not done since February 1996.

My meeting with ACM Sareen seemed to have had the desired effect, because shortly thereafter, Dr Kalam came to Bangalore and constituted a committee called the Performance Verification Committee (PVC), to verify the performance of the FCS during tests on the Iron Bird. He appointed Vice Admiral S.K. Ray as the Chairman of this committee. This committee automatically forced the ADE and HAL Iron Bird teams to work closely together. It was a master stroke by Dr Kalam!

I insisted that I should be present whenever the PVC met. I was therefore made a member of the PVC. We met every Friday afternoon at 1600 hours and reviewed the progress of the Iron Bird tests during the week. Minutes and action points were issued after every meeting. Action taken was reviewed at the following meeting. In this manner, progress of the tests was closely monitored. Over 125 PVC meetings were held over a period of 30 months before we flew TD-1!

Terry Smith, the flight test engineer from Warton, UK, came to NFTC for the second time in late 1998. He was happy with our preparations for first flight especially with the way the two EGR phases had been conducted. He now wanted us to look at all flight safety concerns in great detail, and to prepare an overall safety document which would cover all activities undertaken at NFTC. We started brainstorming about safety issues right away.

After Terry's last visit I had requested Dr Kota to tell HAL (AR&DC) to procure a set of pressure instruments and prepare a scheme to provide an independent source of dynamic and static air pressure for them. No action had been taken, using the excuse that first flight was very far away. Terry reiterated his view that we should have these independent instruments in place before we flew TD-1. I now thumped the table at the weekly PCT meetings till things started moving.

CHAPTER 9

The Iron Bird and Taxi Tests

The Iron Bird is a test rig in which the entire hardware and software of a fly-by-wire FCS is tested and cleared for flight. After the IV&V team had verified the DFCC software, validation had to be now done by checking the functionality of the system against the top level FRD. HAL (AR&DC) was the place where the Iron Bird for the LCA programme was built. It had all the FCS hardware like actuators for all the control surfaces on the aircraft, airbrake actuators, aircraft systems like the hydraulics, electrics, undercarriage, the DFCC, associated test station and a cockpit equipped with the actual control column and throttle as in the aircraft. The cockpit had low fidelity visuals which were not good enough for HQ evaluation, but adequate for checking out the integrated functioning of the FCS under all normal and emergency conditions of flight. The same mathematical flight model of the aircraft which was in the RTS was ported on an AD-100 computer sourced from a US firm called Analogue Devices. Due to US sanctions it was a big challenge to keep this computer serviceable but our engineers were able to do so. The flight model of the aircraft was integrated with the CLAW as in the RTS to enable the Iron Bird to be flown in real time.

The first task was to build the basic facility with reliable sources of hydraulic and electrical power. A special room was built and a lot of cabling put in place. An external hydraulic power pack was positioned outside the room to keep the noise level low. At every stage of the build, personnel from the Directorate of Aeronautical Quality Assurance (DGAQA) checked out the system to ensure that it was being built to proper engineering standards.

Work on the Iron Bird started in 1995, and progressed at a glacial pace for almost two years. We reviewed the progress at the weekly Monday meetings and tried our best to hasten progress. The problem was the attitude of the corporate management of HAL. Under Chairman R.N. Sharma the LCA programme was given stepmotherly treatment. Till he retired, things did not change.

He finally retired in July 1997 and Dr C.G.K. Nair took over as Chairman. Dr Kota had much better rapport with Dr Nair than he had had with R.N. Sharma. The artificial wall erected between HAL and ADA during Sharma's time was dismantled and two dynamic managers were given key responsibilities. Yogesh Kumar, an Additional General Manager from HAL Lucknow, who had been transferred to Bangalore in 1995 took charge of all LCA related activities at AR&DC. Dr Subba Reddy who had come from HAL Nashik in 1987, took charge of Iron Bird development. BAe engineers reviewed the progress at regular intervals.

Results were immediately seen and by the middle of 1998 the Iron Bird was ready for acceptance tests by DGAQA inspectors. All problems noticed on TD-1 during the first set of engine ground runs were attended to and we did a second phase of ground runs in August 1998.

The FCS is closely tied to the avionics system of the aircraft, as all failure warnings are displayed to the pilot on the MFDs in the cockpit. This means the DFCC, display processor and the mission computer had to work harmoniously with each other. Important avionics system components and the mission computer were modelled and integrated into the Iron Bird. We were not able to use the actual mission computer hardware as avionics integration testing was underway at the DAIR at ADE. We had only four mission computers available at that time and they were all being utilized for various testing and qualification activities. The weekly PVC meetings at the Iron Bird and bi-weekly reviews of FCS development work at ADE did help a great deal in keeping track of all that was going on. Unless I was out of town on other work, I never missed these important meetings. It was very easy to get lost in the maze of activities and jargon!

In August 1998, ACM Sareen visited ADA and reviewed the project. He was pleased to learn about the engine ground runs. He made a very good suggestion to go ahead with taxi tests, without waiting for the FCS to be installed on the aircraft. He also recommended that the aircraft should be towed over a set of rumble strips to make all the bits and pieces that had been left behind during construction, fall out. Usually the entire airframe gets tumbled in a rig to clean out the insides before installation of looms and equipment. We had not done this with the TD-1 airframe and so we quickly implemented ACM Sareen's suggestion. The first time we towed the aircraft over the rumble strips and opened the panels at the bottom of the fuselage, a little heap of metal shavings, screws, rivets, bits of wire and cotton waste fell out! We repeated the runs till the muck stopped falling.

ACM Sareen handed over the reins of the IAF to ACM Anil Tipnis on 31 December 1998. ACM Tipnis and I had flown together in the same Mig-21 squadron for four years in the late-1960s and we were good friends. I went to meet him in January 1999, and requested him to send two test pilots and at least one flight test engineer to NFTC as soon as possible. He told me to stay on at ADA and get the LCA into the air as soon as possible! He gave me complete freedom to act as I thought fit in the interest of the project and promised all support.

Before we could think of taxiing the aircraft, another very important activity had to be completed. This was the Structural Coupling Test (SCT). A bit of explanation is required here. The FCS has gyroscopic sensors which pick up aircraft motion around its three axes and feed it back to the control loop. For example, if the aircraft flew into a small air pocket the sensors would pick up the pitching motion and deflect the aircraft control surfaces in the direction required to smoothen out the disturbance. This is fine as long as the controls react only to the flight condition. Unfortunately, the airframe also bends and distorts whenever the aircraft flies through bumpy weather and it is important to prevent the sensors from transmitting these distortions to the control system. The aircraft is suspended by very strong rubber cords and instrumented to record all the structural frequencies that get excited every time the control surfaces are moved. After the control engineers get this SCT data they design digital 'notch filters', which prevent undesirable frequencies from being fed back to the FCS. For this test the aircraft had to be fitted with all on board equipment and weighed accurately, and the CG position calculated. Our Aerostructures group headed by Dr A.R. Upadhya was doing a test of this type for the first time, and a lot of learning was involved. This is where the consultancy agreement with BAe was very useful. Their experts guided our team through this phase step by step and the SCT was completed by the end of 1998.

On 11 January 1999 an Avro 748 aircraft modified with a 24 foot diameter rotodome crashed at Arakonam near Chennai, killing four IAF officers and four DRDO scientists. The Avro was engaged in testing related to the indigenous Airborne Early Warning project being managed by the DRDO's Centre for Airborne Systems at Bangalore. I was very familiar with this particular aircraft as I had done a lot of test flying on it during the initial phase of the project in 1992–3 when I was Commandant, ASTE. ACM Tipnis rang me up the next day and asked me to be the presiding officer of the Court of Inquiry. I was hardly in a position to say no to the CAS, so I was very busy for the next two months with this additional responsibility. The Court was able to pinpoint the precise cause of the accident which had occurred because an inadequately-designed bracket attaching the rotodome to the pylons on the aircraft had broken in the air and caused the rotodome to separate in flight.

On 17 February 1999, TD-1 was ready for its slow speed taxi test. I had the aircraft parked on a level portion of the tarmac at HAL. This was done to quickly stop the aircraft with chocks, in case of problems with the brakes or nose wheel steering (NWS) system. Rajiv Kothiyal started up, released brakes and for the first time TD-1 moved forward under its own power. It was a lovely sight for all of us who were used only to seeing the aircraft standing in the hangar on jacks, most of the time. He gingerly executed a couple of figures of eight, checked the brakes and felt confident to go on the taxi track the next day. The following day he rolled down the West-facing taxi track which has a prominent slope, experienced a problem with the brakes and NWS and had to shut down the aircraft on the taxi track. During prototype development work, one has to be prepared for all sorts of eventualities. As a measure of abundant caution I had insisted that a crash tender follow the aircraft while it was on the ground, along with a set of ground crew in a jeep with a spare wheel, jacks and towing arm, to quickly tow the aircraft away in case of a problem, without blocking the runway and taxi track for long periods of time. Bangalore is a very busy airport and we did not want to disrupt normal civil traffic any more than was required. I felt I was justified in asking for the first test to be conducted on perfectly level ground! In four graded steps we went up to 75 km per hour (kmph) speed which was the limit without the FCS in place. The engineers collected a lot of data on the behaviour of the new brake-by-wire system, and with the help of Kothiyal's comments were able to fine tune it. The whole team developed confidence in the functioning of all on board systems.

By about April 1999 the digital notch filters were integrated with the CLAW. With these filters in place the fixed gain CLAW had to be accepted by the pilots from the HQ point of view. Kothiyal spent long hours in the RTS looking at the effect of various hardware and software failures on the HQ of the aircraft. I went and looked at problems he had noticed and the two of us were able to devise procedures to safely recover the aircraft if such failures did actually occur. This assessment was crucial for safety of the first flight, because the fixed gain CLAW had not been tested during the IFS sessions at Calspan in the USA in 1995 and 1996. The CLAW tested at that time for acceptable HQ, was of the scheduled gain variety. We were able to flash the green light for the first flight CLAW by June 1999. The DFCC software team then got down to coding and integrating it in the computer.

In May–June 1999, units of the Pakistan army occupied some hill features on our side of the Line of Control in the Kargil sector in Jammu & Kashmir, and a shooting conflict erupted. As the conflagration showed signs of spreading, fighter squadrons of the IAF were pressed into action. One of them was 108 Squadron equipped with Mig-21s which I had commanded as a Wing Commander in 1978–80. I was appointed Commodore Commandant of the squadron for a six-year term in 1995 by the then CAS, ACM Kaul. The squadron was operating from Awantipur close to Srinagar and I felt it was my duty to go on a morale boosting visit to the unit while the mini-war raged. I took permission from Air HQ and went to Awantipur in a service aircraft on 4 July 1999 and exhorted the officers and men to perform their duty with courage, sincerity and zeal. The unit personnel appeared to be in good heart and I grabbed an opportunity to go to the Kargil helipad in a casualty evacuation helicopter. As I stepped down from the helicopter at the helipad, an Indian army Brigadier greeted me with the news that our troops had captured Tiger Hill the previous night. I then noticed some puffs of dust being kicked up about 100 yards from where we were standing and on enquiring what it was, the Brigadier told me that the helipad was being shelled! We descended into a bunker to watch the fireworks in relative safety. Helicopter movements were being monitored by an enemy observation post on the ridge line which was the horizon, and our arrival had attracted attention. The helipad was cleverly sited at the base of a craggy outcrop and shells could not land on it unless the terminal phase of a shell's trajectory was vertical. The enemy gunners could not raise their gun barrels to the required elevation, so the shells were landing harmlessly on open ground some distance away. Nevertheless it was disconcerting to come under enemy fire! The short visit to an operational area reminded me that the primary mission of the LCA was to fight wars to defend Indian air space and territory. The aircraft had to get into service soon in an operationally ready state.

On my return to Bangalore a day later, I found DFCC software testing going on in full swing on the Iron Bird. BAe specialists came and reviewed our progress at regular intervals. My friend, Vice Adm. Ray, had retired and his deputy Sathyaraja of ADE started chairing the weekly PVC meetings. Even though he was far junior to me in both age and years of government service, I continued to attend all PVC meetings as before with him in the chair. He was the electronics and software expert, not I. The project was more important than personal ego.

In August 1999, Wg. Cdr. Nambiar, Sqn. Ldr. Banerjee and Sqn. Ldr. M.K.R. Prasad reported to NFTC. I told them to familiarize themselves with all aircraft systems and start assisting Kothiyal in the RTS. I wanted them to be ready for the next phase of testing on the Iron Bird which was called Pilot in Loop (PIL) tests. In this phase the full software in the DFCC including the CLAW was flown by the test pilot in the Iron Bird. The FCS was checked for proper functioning in the flight envelope earmarked for the first block of flights. Emphasis was placed on checking three important aspects of the, FCS (a) the adequacy of hydraulic power to meet the requirement of operating services like the undercarriage and air brakes, while manoeuvring the aircraft with both normal and emergency hydraulic power (b) the correctness and easy accessibility of FCS failure warnings posted on the MFDs, and (c) the behaviour of the FCS when a channel failed in the DFCC. Raveendran put Prasad in charge of all Iron Bird work in which NFTC had to be involved.

In November 1999, we commenced PIL tests on the Iron Bird. This was the first time both engineers and test pilots had the opportunity to see how the FCS functioned as an integrated whole. Not surprisingly, many anomalies were noticed. The first problem we ran into, was with FCS failure warnings which were posted on the MFDs. Once a failure occurred, the warning would promptly appear on the MFD. The problem arose as soon as a second failure occurred. The first warning would disappear and only the second failure warning would be visible to the pilot. The first warning could be recalled on the screen by double clicking a button on the throttle. Even this would have been acceptable had there been a guarantee that only two failures would occur in a mission. Since this was not the case we had to press for a more user-friendly warning system, which entailed quite a lot of software changes in the display processor. Project Director Avionics, P.N.A.P. Rao, said it would take at least three months to implement all the changes demanded by the pilots. I said unless the pilots were happy with all aspects of man-machine interface, we would not be able to proceed with the PIL tests. The second problem we had was with the adequacy of hydraulic power for the FCS under certain failure conditions, which was overcome by modifying piloting procedures.

The third and perhaps the most interesting problem was to assess the behaviour of the FCS as one channel after the other in the DFCC was deliberately failed by the test team. No one knew exactly how the system would behave after each channel failure and the NFTC team, the CLAW team and DFCC design engineers had to first develop a series of tests which would expose as many weaknesses in the system as possible. This was an intellectual task of the highest class and we all enjoyed the experience very much. We ran through this big matrix of tests and asked for software changes as we went along. When we started looking at the third channel failure too closely, I was suddenly reminded of the advice given by our BAe consultant, Weller earlier that year. He had said, given the current level of reliability in electronic systems, a third failure of a quadruplex system was considered a remote possibility which BAe did not cater for. In their company they would rather spend time on other more likely failures in the hydraulic and electrical systems. With this background information I told Kothiyal and Prasad not to waste any more time on that problem.

The PIL tests threw up a requirement for 11 software changes in the DFCC and took a full year to complete.

Wg. Cdr. Raveendran, Sqn. Ldr. Prasad and the three test pilots evolved a system to report faults and keep track of solutions. Within an hour of the end of a session on the Iron Bird, a Request For Action (RFA) proforma would reach the FCS designers and we would go back to fly the Iron Bird only after corrective action had been taken.

In October1999, Dr Kalam demitted office as the SA to RM and became the Principal Scientific Adviser to the Prime Minister with Cabinet rank. The new SA to RM was Dr V.K. Aatre, a renowned electronics engineer, who was already in DRDO as the Chief Controller R&D in charge of electronics development. Dr Aatre started coming for monthly reviews along with Chairman HAL on the third Saturday of every month. These meetings were useful because the interaction between ADA and HAL improved.

Dr Kota called me one morning in January 2000 and said it was time we constituted a Flight Readiness Review Board (FRRB) as FCS testing was going on at full speed, and once that was done we could look forward to first flight of TD-1 in the second half of 2000. FRRB was a concept we had learnt about through our interactions with engineers at the Wright Laboratories in Dayton, Ohio, USA. It consisted of a team of experts who though not part of the design and development team could look at the whole development process and assure the top management of the programme that all was well. We discussed a list of experts who we thought could do a good job of this onerous task. He asked me to be the Chairman of the FRRB, because finally it was my call to say whether the aircraft was fit to fly or not.

On 26 January 2000, I was awarded the Param Vishisht Seva Medal (PVSM) by the President of India for 'distinguished services of an exceptional order'. I was very happy to have been honoured by the President.

At the first sitting of the FRRB we formed teams to look at

six crucial areas. These were the FCS hardware, CLAW, aircraft structures, avionics architecture, airframe-engine integration plus general systems and preparations for flight testing. I requested the members to be ready to present their initial findings at the second sitting in March 2000.

In February 2000 I went to Air HQ to meet ACM Tipnis. I asked him to give me a Mirage 2000 trainer for use at NFTC. I explained to him the very important requirement to keep the test pilots in current flying practice as well as the need to calibrate the air data system of a chosen Mirage 2000 trainer before it could be used as a chase aircraft for TD-1's first block of flights. He sent for the VCAS, Air Marshal Prithvi Singh Brar, who was also an old squadron buddy of mine, and asked him to do the needful. As he was responsible for day-to-day flying in the IAF, Brar expectedly said that Mirage trainers were in short supply and with all sorts of operational commitments in the offing, it would not be possible to spare an aircraft for NFTC. The CAS said 'Just give him what he wants'. Without that kind of intervention at the very top, I would never have managed to get the aircraft I so badly needed for my plans. I next went to the Air Officer Maintenance, AM Janakiraman, another old friend from ASTE days, and asked for maintenance support to keep the aircraft flying at Bangalore. Janaki suggested that the aircraft should be maintained by the Overhaul Division of HAL which was overhauling Mirages for the IAF. He said maintenance costs should be paid out of project funds. He also called all the officers looking after Mirage maintenance problems at Air HQ and in my presence, gave them strict instructions to keep the Mirage airworthy at Bangalore. For the full year the aircraft was at NFTC, we never had any problem in keeping it in flying condition! The Mirage 2000 KT 205 arrived at NFTC in May 2000.

Meanwhile TD-1 was being prepared for the next phase of EGRs. When we ran the engine for the first time in 1998 we had noticed that the Environmental Cooling System (ECS) was not working well enough to adequately cool the avionics bay in the aircraft. This was where a lot of sensitive equipment had been installed and a controlled environment was necessary for their proper functioning. The ECS was modified to take care of this problem, which was most acute when the aircraft was on the ground, because of poor air flow over the heat exchangers which had to cool high temperature air bled from the engine before routing it to the cold air unit.

In March 2000 Rajiv Kothiyal started the engine and shortly thereafter, he reported a burning smell in the cockpit. At the same time, thick black smoke started pouring out from the area behind the cockpit. I was standing next to the aircraft and as soon as I saw this happen I ran and signalled to him to shut down the engine immediately by drawing my hand across my throat. There after the crash crew who were standing by to cope with such problems quickly brought the situation under control.

Dr Kota asked me to head the investigation team and when we opened up the aircraft we were greatly relieved to find the damage was minimal. Some polyurethane insulation had been wrongly wound around a hot duct and had charred. The entire area where the ECS was fitted and the avionics bay was, however, covered with black soot and had to be cleaned thoroughly. We analysed the sequence of events, studied data from telemetry and recommended that we go back to the original state of the ECS before the modification was implemented. All this took about four months, but we did not waste the time by utilizing it to install FCS hardware on the aircraft. Around this time we had a setback because the structures group decided that the wing attachment bolt holes on the fuselage needed to be reworked because of a tolerance problem. The wings had to come off and that meant a delay of at least three months. On top of that, the undercarriage group said they would have to strengthen the main attachment point to clear the aircraft for a sink rate of 10 ft/sec at touch down. Dr Kota asked me whether 9 ft/sec clearance would be acceptable to the pilots. I had a word with the test pilots and they said they would like to have an undercarriage which was cleared to the correct specification which was 10 ft/sec. The dream of flying TD-1 in 2000 slowly began to fade!

In June 2000, I came to know quite by accident that my batch mate Air Marshal M.S. Sekhon was going to become the Air Officer Commanding in Chief (AOC-in-C) of Southern Air Command at Trivandrum on 1 September 2000. As he was junior to me in the IAF, promoting him to the grade of AOC-in-C, which is equivalent to that of a Secretary to the Government of India (GOI), meant that I was being superseded for no fault of mine. There was an irrational view at Air HQ that I was having a 'good time' at Bangalore which happened to be my home town. The fact that I was working on a project which was to deliver a fourth generation fighter for the IAF inventory, and crucial for the long-term interests of the aeronautical industry in India, was conveniently forgotten The only grounds on which an officer could be superseded were either professional incompetence or lack of medical fitness. I did not think I was incompetent because in my 38 years of service up to that point in time, no one had ever told me I was incompetent and I had been promoted in the first list for every selection grade rank. I was medically fit with a flying medical category. I went to ACM Tipnis and told him that as the CAS it was his duty to take up a case with the GOI and make sure I was also promoted to the grade of AOC-in-C while I continued to be on deputation to ADA. He was taken aback by my request and said it would not be possible for him to do so because I was on deputation to ADA and my case should be taken up by DG ADA, Dr V.K. Aatre. When I went to Dr Aatre, he said that as I was on the strength of the IAF, only the IAF could promote me, and not ADA or DRDO. Back I went to ACM Tipnis and said it was up to him to redress my very genuine grievance. With great reluctance he promised to do 'something'!

In June 2000 a team of BAe FCS specialists came down and reviewed all the work done on the Iron Bird up to that point in time. At the final meeting before their return to the UK, the team leader Dave Allison said 'We have looked at all that you have done and there is nothing more that we can teach you. It is up to you to pluck up courage and fly this aircraft'. I then requested the BAe team to send a test pilot and flight test engineer Terry Smith to review our preparations for flight testing the aircraft, especially the crucial first block of flights. They said they would convey my request to their management.

A couple of weeks later, BAe, who had helped us so much in the development of the FCS, sent me a message that due to pressure of work in the Eurofighter programme it was not possible to send either a test pilot or a flight test engineer to review our preparations for first flight. This was an unexpected setback because BAe had stood by their commitments even after the Pokharan blasts. With no support from Lockheed Martin for the development of the DFCC, no support from GE for the engine, and now with no one to review our preparations for first flight, we were well and truly alone! The sense of isolation only steeled our resolve to succeed with the technology demonstration phase of the LCA programme.

I had decided that Rajiv Kothiyal would pilot TD-1 for the first flight and Nambiar would be the standby pilot. This meant both pilots had to be brought to an identical level of training in terms of familiarity with the aircraft's systems, and HQ. Both had to be equally at home in the cockpit and have the knowledge and ability to handle all emergencies. I told Banerjee he would be flying the chase Mirage 2000. All three test pilots and the two flight test engineers started flying the Mirage 2000 regularly. Whenever I got fed up of attending meetings, I too flew the Mirage 2000, with one or the other of the three test pilots.

Apart from flying practice for the test pilots the team had three important tasks to perform. First, they had to calibrate the air data system of the Mirage 2000 and find out the accuracy of the speed and altitude indications shown to the pilot in the cockpit. Only then could the Mirage 2000 be used as a standard to check the accuracy of the air data system of TD-1. They evolved a test technique which used the satellite-based GPS signals to carry out this calibration which was completed by August 2000. This had not been done before in India, so NFTC became a trail blazer of sorts. The second task was to evolve procedures for the chase aircraft to follow when TD-1 started flying. Every detail from engine start, taxi, take off, climb, flight test manoeuvres, descent, approach, landing, taxi back to dispersal and engine shut down, was covered by these procedures. The third and equally important task was to establish radio communication protocols between the test aircraft, chase aircraft, the test director, the ATC tower at Bangalore, the ATC tower at Yelahanka which was the diversionary airfield, the surveillance radar at Bangalore, rescue helicopter crew and crash crew. With so many agencies involved in each flight there could be no room for confusion. These protocols were written down and circulated to all concerned to ensure total clarity in communications between the various agencies.

CHAPTER 10

The Patna Air Crash and Preparations for First Flight

While we were all working at a feverish pace to achieve first flight of TD-1 by the end of 2000, an Alliance Air Boeing 737-200 with 53 persons on board crashed at Patna on 17 July 2000. The aircraft was on the final approach to land at Lok Nayak Jayaprakash Narayan International Airport at Patna when it suddenly lost height, veered to the left of the approach path, and crashed in the middle of a residential area called Gardani Bagh. Several houses were damaged; some civilians were killed on the ground and only four passengers survived. The Union Minister for Civil Aviation, Shri Sharad Yadav, rushed to the scene of the accident and made a statement that an inquiry into the cause of the accident would be conducted by a sitting judge of the Patna High Court. The Chief Justice of the Patna High Court, Justice Ravi Dhawan, said he would not be able to spare a judge for the inquiry because of pressure of work in the High Court, and more importantly, because he thought the accident should be inquired into by an aviation professional, and not a judge. In spite of a lot of pressure from the Ministry of Civil Aviation, he stuck to his guns and a court of inquiry was not constituted for three whole weeks. The print and electronic media went wild with allegations of a cover up. Having conducted an enquiry for the DGCA after an Indian Airlines Dornier 228 crash in Kochi, in July 1998, I had a sneaking suspicion that the enquiry would be thrust upon me!

On 8 August 2000, my 59th birthday, I did get a call from H.S. Khola, the Director-General of Civil Aviation, requesting me to head the Court of Inquiry. I immediately said I would not be able to work full-time on the inquiry as I had my hands full trying to get the LCA off the ground. He said I could work in any manner I thought fit, without prejudice to my primary responsibility at ADA, but that I should not refuse to head the inquiry. I told him to ask the SA to RM, Dr V.K. Aatre, as well as the CAS ACM Tipnis, whether they were willing to spare me. A short while later he called back saying that the Secretary, Civil Aviation, A.H. Jung, had obtained permission from the MOD to utilize my services. I visited the site of the crash on 11 August 2000, examined the wreckage, had the two engines and the Crash Data Recorder (CDR) despatched to Air India, Mumbai for strip examination and data extraction. I came back to Bangalore in time for another series of EGRs on TD-1. Thereafter, I held three days of public hearings at Patna and examined a number of witnesses. By devoting about a week of effort every month towards the inquiry, and thanks to cell phones, I was able to do justice to both jobs but I was a really busy man for about seven months.

At the RTS we started working on the flight profile for the first flight of TD-1. Dr Srinath Kumar of the CLAW team did not want to fly the aircraft with too much of aerodynamic instability, especially with fixed gains, and so Dr Kota felt we should use ballast in the nose of the aircraft to move the CG forward. Keeping the wing fuel tanks empty also helped to keep the CG forward. The flight test team decided to have only 1800 kg of fuel at start up (wing tanks partially full) for the first block of 12 flights. About 400 kg of fuel would be consumed during the 30 to 45 minutes on ground before take-off and the wing tanks would be empty. Fortunately for us Dr K.V.L. Rao, PD (Propulsion), had had the foresight to obtain a very accurate mathematical thrust model of the GE F404 F2J3 engine from GE at Lynn, Massachusetts, USA, well before sanctions were imposed. When we integrated this model in the RTS we found a close match between predicted performance and actual performance in the simulator. With this confidence in the engine model we carefully looked at fuel consumed during various profiles and chose the most conservative one for first flight. Due to the fact that first flight would be flown with the wing tanks empty, this profile was for only 18 minutes, but the pilot would have adequate fuel to divert to Yelahanka if the need arose. Duration of first flight did not matter because the only aim of the first flight of a prototype is to execute a safe landing! I made all the three test pilots practise this profile till they could fly it while asleep!

The Alliance Air Boeing's CDR data showed that the crash was due to human error of the aircrew. I was given the powers of a judge under the Indian Aircraft Act 1934 for the duration of the enquiry, and made full use of those powers. I opened a website and put out all the evidence I collected on it. When people visiting the site saw the track flown by the aircraft before it crashed they could see for themselves the errors committed by the pilots. Though we knew the cause of the accident I had to conduct three more days of public hearings at Delhi, visit the Boeing plant at Seattle, USA, and have some of the control system actuators strip examined, at the manufacturer's plant at Los Angeles, USA. When I submitted the final report in March 2001 to Shri Sharad Yadav, the Union Minister for Civil Aviation, he ordered it to be released on the website immediately. I expected aviation professionals from around the world to pick holes in my report but I did not get a single query from any one. Transparency of the investigative process certainly has its merits! Since new norms of transparency were established in the course of this investigation, I am sure the public will accept nothing less, in any future enquiry of this nature.

In October 2000, when we thought we were about eight weeks away from first flight, all of us at ADA got a very rude shock. The chief of integration activities on the aircraft in the prototype hangar at HAL was an Additional General Manager, M.K. Govind. He had performed this extremely important and difficult task with great professional competence for three years and we had come to rely a lot on his judgement and experience. Without informing anyone at ADA, HAL's top management decided to transfer Govind to head the BAe-HAL software joint venture. When I first heard of this development, I went to Govind in the hangar and asked him whether he was keen on the move. He said his first love was the LCA project but he could not go against the wishes of his management. Both Dr Kota and I requested Dr C.G.K. Nair, Chairman HAL, not to move Govind out at this critical stage of integration activities, just a few weeks before first flight of this complex prototype. He said he was not able to find anyone suitable to head the BAe-HAL software venture except Govind, and we were faced with a crisis. All the PDs at ADA worked long hours assisting the new chief of integration, Sriramachandra Rao, Govind's former deputy, to get up to speed. By putting in this extra effort we were able to manage the risk caused by the sudden departure of Govind from the scene.

Later that month Sheila and I went to Delhi to attend an investiture ceremony at Rashtrapati Bhavan, where I was to receive my PVSM from President K.R. Narayanan. At a lunch at Air House the following day, ACM Tipnis called me aside and said the GOI was not willing to promote me to the grade of AOC-in-C. I said it was the responsibility of Air HQ to fight this battle to see that justice was done and left it at that.

I returned from a 10-day visit to the USA, in connection with the Alliance Air Boeing crash inquiry, in the first week of November 2000 and found TD-1 still being worked upon in the hangar. The PIL tests on the Iron Bird had been completed and I reviewed every result along with the pilots and engineers, and was pleasantly surprised by the level of confidence the three test pilots had developed in the fly by wire FCS.

From the flight test point of view we had one more task which was to fly the Iron Bird for 50 hours, to satisfy ourselves that the system could actually operate for that length of time without experiencing a single failure. I insisted that if a failure occurred even after 49 hours and 59 minutes we would have to reset the clock to zero and start all over again! I also insisted that for the first block of flights we would only use the DFCC which had completed the 50 hours fault-free run test.

Before TD-1 could fly, an administrative problem cropped up. All aircraft in India have to be licensed to fly either by the DGCA or the Ministry of Defence. TD-1 had to fly with IAF roundels painted on it and needed an alpha numeric registration number. I rang up ACM Tipnis and suggested that the number for TD-1 should be KH-2001. The letters KH were in honour of Dr Kota Harinarayana, who by any yardstick was the man responsible for bringing the project to the stage of first flight in the face of formidable odds. 2001 would represent the year of first flight because by now it was clear we would not be able to do it in 2000. The CAS said as the aircraft was not borne on the IAF inventory he could not agree to IAF roundels being painted on it. I had to explain to him the need for the aircraft to fly under IAF colours. He finally said I could do whatever I thought fit. Without further ado I went to the hangar and told the paint shop to paint IAF roundels and KH 2001 on TD-1 and informed Dr Kota later.

Around the second week of December 2000, TD-1 emerged from the hangar ready for the last round of tests before it could be handed over to NFTC for the final taxi trials. As the aircraft was packed with electrical and electronic equipment the engineers had to carry out a large number of tests called Electro Magnetic Interference (EMI) and Electro Magnetic Compatibility (EMC) checks. A series of tests were done to prove, that all on board systems, especially the FCS, functioned in harmony without interfering with each other. These tests were satisfactory. In the second series of tests the aircraft was illuminated with electromagnetic radiation at various frequencies, which the engineers had ascertained by analysis could be problematic. No interference was observed in any system. I was worried about the effect of the powerful ATC surveillance radar at the airfield. As TD-1 took off, it would have to fly through the lobe of the radar at a distance of only 500 metres. I requested the specialists to look at this problem. They measured the electromagnetic field strength on the runway in front of the ATC and said it was safe. My second worry was the effect of the Mirage 2000's radar on TD-1. As it would be flying close to TD-1 while chasing it we had to see the effect of its radar on the prototype. We had TD-1 parked at the parking bay. Late one evening, when there was not much civil traffic at the airfield, Nambiar started the engine, turned on all the systems and Banerjee illuminated it with the Mirage's radar from a distance of only 20 metres. There was no interference noticed in any system. EMI/EMC tests were satisfactory and we were ready for the final lap leading to first flight.

Before a prototype can take to the air, the certification agency, CEMILAC in this case, had to satisfy itself that the aircraft had been developed according to accepted international aeronautical standards of design and development. Nagraj, CE CEMILAC and his team studied over 1000 design documents, and a large number of test reports to be able to clear the aircraft to fly. This process took almost a year to complete and was done in parallel with the FRRB. I was reminded of the saying in aeronautical circles, that an aircraft, would be ready for first flight only when the weight of documentation equalled the weight of the aircraft, which in this case was six tons!

The Directorate General of Aeronautical Quality Assurance (DGAQA) had to satisfy itself that the aircraft had been manufactured to internationally accepted standards. Representatives of CEMILAC and DGAQA involved themselves fully in the design, development and manufacture of the prototype to be able to say that all was well. After satisfying themselves CEMILAC issued a Flight Clearance Note (FCN) in which the aircraft was cleared for flight subject to the limitations specified in the note. The DGAQA representative signed the release for flight form, after a final check out of the aircraft before it was moved to the flight line.

We did two EGRs on 14 December 2000, and planned two low speed taxi runs, one each by Kothiyal and Nambiar. On

18 December 2000, Nambiar went up to 150 kmph. Design predictions said TD-1 would take-off at a speed of about 260 kmph. To go beyond 200 kmph we needed to have the aircraft cleared to fly by CEMILAC and the FRRB as there was always a chance of an unplanned lift off during high speed taxy tests. On 23 December 2000, Kothiyal went up to 200 kmph and TD-1 behaved perfectly. CEMILAC had issued the FCN. It was time to convene the FRRB for its fifth and final sitting. We had alerted all the members about the possibility of the final session being held on 24 December 2000. I rang up ACM Tipnis and requested him to attend the final session. He flew down and invited me to have dinner with him at the HQ Training Command mess on 23 December 2000. When I met him there he said 'My advisers have told me not to attend the FRRB as it would indicate IAF support for the programme. What do you suggest?' I said 'Sir, the LCA is being built only for the Indian Air Force and not for an enemy air force. Please come'. He came for the meeting.

The conference hall at ADA was crammed with people when the FRRB began its final session. I was in the chair. Apart from other members of the FRRB, ACM Tipnis, CAS, Air Marshal J.S. Rai, AOC-in-C Training Command, Dr V.K. Aatre, DG ADA, Dr Kota Harinarayana, Programme Director LCA, Nagraj CE, CEMILAC, Mahajan, Regional Director DGAQA, Dr. K.G. Narayanan, Director ADE, Behari Lal, Offg Chairman HAL, Yogesh Kumar, GM AR&DC, HAL, Wg. Cdr. Rakesh Sharma, CTP, HAL, all PDs at ADA, and NFTC pilots and engineers were present. Prominent experts from other organizations who were members of the FRRB were Dr B.N. Suresh, Head of the Controls Division, Vikram Sarabhai Space Centre, Trivandrum, K.V.S.S, Prasad Rao, Director, Research Centre Immarat, Hyderabad, Professor K.P. Rao, Head of Structures, Department of Aerospace Engineering, Indian Institute of Science (IISc) and Professor Nagabhushna, Department of Electrical Engineering, IISc. The six groups which were asked to look at the development process in depth in each of their disciplines, presented their findings to the full board. Dr B.N. Suresh whose group had looked into the development of the fly-by-wire FCS said he was satisfied that the system had been developed according to existing technical standards. K.V.S.S. Prasad Rao confirmed that all on board software had been properly verified and validated. Professor K.P. Rao said the airframe was structurally sound and Professor Nagabhushna stated that the electrical grounding in the aircraft and EMC of various on board systems were satisfactory. This took about two hours. All the group leaders said they had no doubt about the readiness of TD-1 to fly. I then threw the meeting open for discussion. A few members started raising all kinds of doubts which I felt were not germane to clearing the aircraft for flight. After a few minutes I felt it was time to bite the bullet. I applied the guillotine to the discussion. I said, 'Gentlemen, we have spoken enough. We have looked at all aspects of design and manufacture of this aircraft for the past year. All on board systems have performed satisfactorily during the slow speed taxi tests. Kothiyal and Nambiar are happy with the way the aircraft has behaved up to 200 kmph. The FRRB clears TD-1 for high speed taxi runs leading to first flight. The meeting is closed.' I got up from my chair and started walking out of the hall. There was stunned silence for a few moments and then a babble of excited voices broke out. Everyone knew we had taken an irrevocable step. We had to fly TD-1! We had taken this momentous decision based only on our own professional confidence with no inputs from any foreign consultant. The biggest benefit of the US sanctions was what I have termed the 'indigenization of decision-making'. It was one of the unforgettable moments of my career.

I got a call from ACM Tipnis the next working day. He sounded very upset. 'What sort of a flight clearance meeting was that you chaired? Nothing was said about in-flight emergencies or how the first flight would take place. And the person who reviewed the flight controls never said any thing about how the aircraft would behave in the air.' I immediately understood the problem. I explained to him that all that he had mentioned would be covered in the first flight briefing which would take place just before the flight. I said I would invite him for that as well.

I had instituted a system of briefing and debriefing before and after every EGR and taxi test. All involved in the day's activities would attend these briefings and debriefings. The test director would conduct the briefing. The test pilot had to submit a written 'hot' report which would give an accurate account of all that he had experienced during the test. This report was written immediately after he returned to his room after the test while events were still fresh in his mind. The test director and the engineers at the monitoring consoles, would then present what they had seen in real time during the test. They could refer to all telemetered data which had been recorded and stored. The next day a detailed debriefing would be held after the designers had looked at the flight test data recorded on board the aircraft. I did not permit any deviation from this system of briefings and debriefings. This approach helped the NFTC team to keep track of all flight test activities undertaken.

One more critical test was left which was to raise the nose wheel at 240 kmph. This would be the first time we would be exercising the control surfaces on the aircraft while the aircraft was rolling at high speed on the runway. As a measure of abundant precaution, we had decided to throttle the engine back to idle before raising the nose wheel. This was done to reduce the chances of an inadvertent lift off. On 28 December 2000, Kothiyal reached a speed of 250 kmph on the runway, throttled the engine back to idle and raised the nose wheel at 240 kmph. The nose rose exactly as expected and he stopped the aircraft using only the brakes. At the debriefing we looked at the telemetered data especially of the FCS and at the behaviour of all onboard systems. Everything had worked satisfactorily. Kothiyal said he was happy with the way the aircraft as a whole had behaved but wanted to repeat the test and use the tail chute to slow the aircraft before commencing braking. On the afternoon of 31 December 2000,

Kothiyal repeated the test and stopped the aircraft using the tail chute. Dr K.G. Narayanan had come for the debriefing. Again all on board systems had worked satisfactorily. I said, 'On the last day of the year just a few hours before the new millennium I pronounce that TD-1 is ready for first flight'. That is how close we came to flying TD-1 in the year 2000! That night Sheila and I went to the New Year ball at the Bangalore Club and enjoyed ourselves, though I knew great trials lay ahead.

The next morning I went to Mrs Mercy Mathew of the India Meteorological Department at the airport and asked her what the weather would be like over the next few days. She showed me the latest satellite picture and said there was a weather system approaching Bangalore from the Bay of Bengal which would cause clouding in the morning hours for the next 48 hours. I asked her whether 4 January 2001 would be free of cloud cover, as I wanted absolutely clear skies for the first flight. She assured me that the day would have fine weather. I went back to my office, called ACM Tipnis and told him first flight of TD-1 was now planned for 4 January 2001. He said he would like to fly in the chase aircraft and would be in Bangalore by the previous evening. I requested him to tell the Operations staff to position one more Mirage 2000 as the second chase aircraft. I did not want to alter the duties of the main chase Mirage 2000, which would be flown by Nambiar who had very specific and important duties to perform like calling out speed checks to Kothiyal and giving him advice in the event of an in flight emergency. The rear seat pilot, Sqn. Ldr. Suneet Krishna, was given the job of videographing the entire flight from take-off to landing. I told Tarun Banerjee to fly the second Mirage 2000 with the CAS occupying the rear seat.

On 2 and 3 January 2001, the NFTC was a hive of activity. The IAF base at Yelahanka was the main diversionary airfield where Kothiyal and Nambiar had practised approaches in the Mirage 2000. Now there was a need for a final briefing for the rescue and fire services personnel there. HAL and the

NFTC personnel went and briefed them about the rescue procedures for pilots trapped in the LCA or Mirage 2000 cockpits, should an emergency landing take place at the diversion. A crash trolley with LCA and Mirage 2000 towing equipment and spare wheels was positioned at Yelahanka.

I went to meet the AOC-in-C Training Command, Air Marshal J.S. Rai, and requested him to position two Mi-8 helicopters at ASTE on 3 January 2001, for Search and Rescue (SAR) duties. One of them would be on airborne standby with a stretcher and medical team on board and the other would be on standby on the ground. One Chetak helicopter from ASTE would also be on airborne standby for SAR duties with an aerospace medical specialist from the Institute of Aerospace Medicine, Bangalore on board. With the benefit of hindsight, all this may seem like overkill but, believe me, at that time everyone felt it was necessary for obvious reasons!

We were unable to satisfactorily simulate the last stage of landing in the RTS. Even after the engine had been throttled back to idle at flare out, the aircraft floated for a long time before touching down. This was contrary to real world experience wherein delta-winged aircraft sank and touched down as soon as the engine was throttled back to idle. Long ago I had told Kothiyal, Nambiar and Banerjee that they should not worry about this shortcoming of the RTS, as in actual fact the LCA would behave exactly like the Mirage 2000, because both were delta-winged aircraft and would therefore exhibit similar characteristics during the flare out and touchdown. They had been flying the Mirage 2000 regularly during the past six months. The time had come for Kothiyal to practise his approaches, flare outs and touchdowns on that aircraft some more times, till he was absolutely confident of executing the landing on TD-1. On 3 January 2001, Kothiyal and Nambiar went to the RTS in the morning and practised the first flight profile and emergency procedures. In the afternoon Kothiyal flew the Mirage 2000 with Banerjee in the back seat and practised the approach and landing phase till he was satisfied. We held a round of discussions with the telemetry monitoring console personnel and reviewed emergency procedures with them. At the end of that day I was finally confident we would be able to carry out a safe first flight of TD-1 the following morning.

ACM Tipnis arrived in the evening and I went to the HQ Training Command mess to brief him about the following day's sequence of events. I requested him to be at NFTC by 0745 hours the next morning. I then called my friends AM S. Krishnaswamy, AOC-in-C Western Air Command in Delhi, and AM Vinod Patney, VCAS at Air HQ about the impending first flight. Both of them wished me luck and said they were very sure all would turn out well. It felt good to be reassured by old friends.

From all I have said it should be clear that the successful first flight of TD-1 was achieved by meticulous attention to detail with nothing left to chance. It was all about risk management and self confidence and had taken 75 months of unremitting effort by the NFTC. The sanctions imposed by the USA were in place for 31 months preceding the first flight of TD-1. We had 'flown' 1000 hours on the RTS during which we had defined the fixed gain flight envelope, carried out 2000 landings, done 336 landings during IFS, executed 37 EGRs, 17 taxi tests, 92 sorties on the Mirage 2000 trainer, for pilot training and flight test technique development, attended over 1000 meetings with the design groups, developed the Pilots Manual and operating procedures both normal and emergency. In addition the NFTC test pilots and flight test engineers had made a significant contribution to the development of the RTS and three crucial ground test rigs, the CEF, the DAIR, the Iron Bird, spending considerable time 'flying' these ground rigs, validating avionics and FCS software. The analysis team had developed the entire software for the displays at the telemetry monitoring station. Clearly this magnitude of intensely focused effort would not have been possible without a small but dedicated flight test team looking exclusively at the LCA programme.

CHAPTER 11

Honours and Awards, Aero India 2001 and Completion of the First Block of Flights

After the celebrations at the parking area were over we assembled in the conference hall of NFTC for the debriefing. In my presence, the Raksha Mantri George Fernandes told Dr Aatre to send the citations of deserving personnel for awards to him soon. I was very clear in my mind that Kothiyal deserved an award for the courage of having undertaken the risky first flight of a high technology prototype. I decided to recommend him for the award of the Kirti Chakra, the second highest award for courage in peacetime. Dr Kota agreed with me and I despatched his citation to Air HQ so that the award could be announced by Republic Day, 26 January 2001.

ACM Tipnis called me on 5 January 2001. He congratulated me for the military precision with which the programme of the previous day had unfolded and the flawless first flight of TD-1 and asked me to convey his appreciation to all concerned. I told him that I had sent a citation for the award of the Kirti Chakra to Kothiyal. He said he did not agree with me and that he would recommend him only for an Ati Vishisht Seva Medal (AVSM) which is an award for meritorious service only. I said an AVSM did not recognize the courage displayed by Kothiyal and stoutly defended my recommendation. ACM Tipnis did not agree and rang off.

On 21 January 2001, Dr Kota and I met ACM Tipnis at the Annual General Meeting of the Aeronautical Society of India at Agra. We both went up to him and said Kothiyal deserved nothing less than a Kirti Chakra and made him change his mind. On 26 January 2001, I scanned the morning papers to see which award Dr Kota had been conferred with. I was expecting him to be awarded the Padma Bhushan. To my utter horror I found he had not been given any recognition for his stupendous effort over a period of 15 years. This was a pity because, like justice, recognition delayed was recognition denied. Kothiyal had been awarded the Kirti Chakra and Dr C.G.K. Nair, Chairman HAL, the Padma Shree.

Over the next two years Dr Kota, Dr K.G. Narayanan, Dr Srinath Kumar and nine prominent members of the CLAW team, Yogesh Kumar and Dr Subba Reddy of HAL AR&DC, received recognition from DRDO and professional Societies like the Aeronautical Society of India. Dr Kota was awarded the Padma Shree by the President of India on 26 January 2002. Dr K.G. Narayanan and Dr Kota were given the DRDO award for Technology Development. Some of the PDs from ADA also received recognition of some sort or the other.

There was a lot of euphoria in the press about the successful flight of TD-1. I knew the enormous amount of ground that had to be covered before the LCA could enter IAF service, as a ready-to-go-to-war machine. I harboured a fear of a different sort. Would Team LCA start breaking up? A fairly large number of people who had worked in the programme thought their job was done with the first flight of TD-1! I was very clear in my mind that the same enthusiasm and zeal with which Team LCA had approached first flight would have to be sustained for at least a decade and a half, before the LCA fitted with a Kaveri engine and an indigenous MMR could enter service as an operational fighter. At every opportunity I got to speak to members of Team LCA, I cautioned them that we had mountains to climb. I kept telling them that the biggest challenges in the programme were ahead of us and not behind! Unfortunately my worst fears were soon realized and a lot of important players from ADA, ADE and HAL left for greener pastures. It just so happened that the influx into Bangalore of multi-national companies started in 2000 and anyone who had worked in the LCA programme was very attractive prey for head hunters. The biggest beneficiaries were companies like GE, Honeywell, GM, Microsoft, Dell, Infosys and Wipro.

Coming back to the story of the first block of flights, when we looked at the flight test data of the first flight carefully, we found that the temperature in the battery compartment in the nose bay of the aircraft had gone up to a higher than expected value. A hot air duct of the ECS had to be rerouted and the FCS and CLAW teams wanted to sift through reams of data and satisfy themselves that all was well. All this work took over three weeks and we did the second flight of TD-1 on 28 January 2001. During this flight, Kothiyal cycled the undercarriage for the first time in the air and there was no hitch. In early February, we did the third flight and felt we could do a brief flypast on the opening day of Aero India 2001 on 7 February 2001. Kothiyal practised the profile in the RTS, worked out the flying time required from start up to landing, and the fuel figures at each stage of the flight. I sent the instrumentation engineers to Yelahanka to set-up a telemetry relay station so that we could continuously monitor the flight from the monitoring room. Due to a last minute problem with the PBIT of the FCS, we were not able to take part in the inaugural flypast.

We managed to sort the problem out and asked the air show organizers to give us a slot during the flying display on the afternoon of 10 February 2001 to do just a brief straight and level fly by at 150 metres AGL. I went to the air show in the morning and was having lunch at the DRDO chalet around 1 p.m. when Dr Kota came up to me and said the DGAQA inspector at HAL was not clearing the aircraft because pilot oxygen contents were low. Could I go and take a look? It was already past 1 p.m. and I knew Kothiyal had to start up by 2.15 p.m. to make the allotted time of 3.10 p.m. for the fly by. I drove at break neck speed back to the tarmac at HAL and found Kothiyal all strapped up in TD-1, ready to start the engine. Jayavelu, the DGAQA inspector was standing on the cockpit ladder holding the release for flight form. It was 2:20

p.m. I spoke to him and found that because pilot oxygen contents were low he wanted the liquid oxygen (LOX) container in the aircraft to be charged to the full. According to the rule book he was right. No LOX was available as the tanker had gone to the factory to pick up a fresh supply. Kothiyal was willing to overlook the slight deficiency as the flight duration was for only 15 minutes, all at a height below 5000 ft AMSL. I looked at the contents gauge and though it was not full I knew it would last for at least 45 minutes of normal use. There was no risk involved, but the inspector did not want to be held responsible if anything untoward occurred, so he wanted me to be party to the decision. I told Jayavelu to clear the flight and Kothiyal was able to display TD-1 to an eagerly waiting crowd at Yelahanka albeit for only 30 seconds! The next morning all major dailies in the country carried a lovely photograph of TD-1 in flight. As far as I was concerned it was important to garner political support for the programme and TD-1's appearance at Aero India 2001 certainly gave us a lot of positive publicity. I was later criticized by some of my friends for taking an unnecessary risk by flying a prototype at an international air show, on just its fourth flight, but my judgement was that the risk was well within acceptable limits.

The first prototype airframe PV-1 was brought to the flight hangar for equipping in February 2001.We had the three aircrafts TD-1, TD-2 and PV-1 parked side by side and photographed. I told everyone that I would be far happier if I could see all three in the air at the same time!

About this time the avionics design group at ADA took a decision to change the avionics architecture for the fourth aircraft PV-2. It was decided to develop a new open architecture Mission Computer and a full glass cockpit with three MFDs instead of two as in the TDs. This would bring the man-machine interface of the LCA at par with similar fourth generation fighters in the world.

The empty weight of the two TDs was more than the target weight and a major exercise was launched to reduce weight by increasing the use of composites in the airframe. The weight reduction exercise was to take effect from PV-2 onwards.

By the end of March 2001, Kothiyal had flown six flights and Nambiar was getting impatient to fly TD-1. As he had been fully trained to undertake even the first flight had circumstances warranted it, I had no hesitation in letting him fly from the seventh flight onwards. On the seventh flight we ran into a problem with the nose wheel. On the landing roll he had felt a shimmy which also showed up in the flight test data. The undercarriage group at HAL tried out various fixes and both pilots carried out a number of taxi tests but the problem persisted. By the time it was satisfactorily resolved, it was May 2001. With fixed gains in the FCS we could go only up to M 0.7 and we felt we would have enough data to calibrate the air data system up to that speed in about a dozen flights. On 2 June 2001, on the twelfth flight, Nambiar did some tower fly by runs at a height of 100 metres AGL at various speeds. We now had enough data to calibrate the air data system. Dr Kota felt we should stop flying TD-1 at that stage as the workforce in the hangar had to shift their attention to TD-2 which was scheduled to fly nine months after TD-1 in September 2001. TD-1 itself had to be worked on, to make the slats and airbrakes operational, and the fuel system fit to carry full internal fuel for the next block of flights. I agreed to his suggestion, and TD-1 was grounded though we did some more taxi tests in June to rectify problems with the brake management and nose wheel steering systems. Dr Kota and I addressed a press conference and announced the successful completion of the first block of 12 flights of the technology demonstration programme. I told the press that both the test pilots who had flown the aircraft were very pleased with its FCS and HQ. In other words the quadruplex digital fly-by-wire FCS had behaved very satisfactorily.

In early 1961, the HF-24 Marut prototype was extensively damaged due to an aborted take-off on its attempted first flight. In 1974, the US Navy fighter F-14 Tomcat crashed on its first flight due to a double hydraulic failure. In the mid-1980s the Swedish Gripen programme lost two prototypes within the first year of commencement of flight tests. In fact the first crash took place during the fifth flight of the first prototype. In the 1990s the F-22 Raptor programme in the United States also lost a prototype very early in the programme. Had the LCA programme suffered even a single serious incident the media and a fair number of politicians and some in the GOI would have bayed for closure of the project! For us in the flight test team failure was, therefore, not an option.

At the NFTC we had introduced the system of drawing up a test schedule for every sortie, converting it into a flight profile and fine tuning it by flying it in the RTS. The fidelity of the RTS allowed us to accurately note the time taken and fuel consumed to fly every segment of the profile. This in turn enabled the test director at the monitoring console, to track the test sortie very carefully, and the test pilot to execute test manoeuvres with the required precision as he would have practised it adequately before doing it in the air. Productivity of each test sortie went up and we were able to accomplish all that was required to be done with very few abortive sorties. Flight safety also improved because the test director and the test pilot had prior knowledge of areas where they might run into trouble. In addition we used the Mirage 2000 as a chase aircraft for all the 12 fights of the first block. This was the first time in the country that a prototype's flight test programme had been monitored with such rigour.

After the detailed debriefing after each sortie was conducted, the NFTC raised a RFA proforma giving a description of the anomalies in HQ, or in various systems noticed during the sortie. This would be circulated to all departments concerned at ADA, HAL, ADE and the CLAW team. One FTE at the NFTC kept track of all RFAs and the remedial action taken. A RFA was 'closed' only after the corrective action taken by the designers was cleared by the test pilots and engineers from the user point of view.

Dr Kota had spent 15 years steering the LCA programme

under the most adverse circumstances and it was only due to his dogged determination and perseverance that the programme had reached this stage. The only upward movement he could look forward to was to become DG ADA. It would have been in the fitness of things had he been elevated to that position. Unfortunately he was denied that slot. He came to my office at NFTC one morning and said he would be leaving ADA and had recommended to Dr Aatre that I be made DG ADA. I said I would be 60 years old on 8 August 2001, and would be retiring at the end of that month. He said I could stay on for at least two more years till the age of 62. I had no doubt in my mind that I would be able to do genuine justice to the job, as I was in a knowledgeable position as far as managing a fighter aircraft development programme was concerned. Being a realist, I was in a position to take practical, as opposed to emotional, programme decisions to accelerate the entry of the aircraft into service.

Dr Aatre came to Bangalore a few days later, to say Dr Kota would be leaving ADA shortly, and asked me to oversee all activities of ADA for two years while he remained DG ADA. He said he would create a post of Director ADA who would be slotted in between the Programme Director and DG ADA. I agreed to stay on as it would enable me to contribute to the LCA programme for two more years.

Nothing was happening as far as my promotion to the grade of AOC-in-C was concerned. I was running out of time as superannuation was only 75 days away! In the middle of June 2001 I went to Pathankot on my farewell visit as Commodore Commandant to 108 Squadron. On my way back I stopped over at Delhi and met ACM Tipnis in his office. He said the GOI was yet to decide my case and he could offer me very little hope. I had sought legal advice before I left Bangalore and the lawyer had advised me to file a writ petition in the Karnataka High Court as there was no way the GOI could deny me my promotion after having promoted someone junior to me. I told the CAS that he was compelling me to take recourse to legal action. He was taken aback and in my presence rang up the Defence Secretary, Yogendra Narain, and asked him about my case. Mr Narain sounded more hopeful and said he would do his best to see that justice was done. I again reminded the CAS that it was his responsibility to pursue my case and that I had no intention of dragging Air HQ to court.

I went to the hangar frequently to keep track of the work going on TD-2 and came to the sad conclusion that it would not fly before the end of 2001. Around this time the GOI sanctioned development of the Intermediate Jet Trainer (IJT) to HAL (AR&DC). I knew immediately that the IJT programme would adversely impact the LCA programme because the workforce was limited, and the same team leaders would have to oversee work on both projects. ADA had committed themselves to complete the technology demonstration programme of 220 flights by December 2003 which was only 17 months away. In this time-frame it would not be possible to train and deploy at least 100 more technicians, which number I assessed was the minimum required to push both projects simultaneously.

My 60th birthday was on 8 August 2001. I was reminded of poet John Milton's lines 'How soon hath Time, the subtle thief of youth, stolen on his wing my three and twentieth year'. I went to the ASTE across the runway from my office, and flew a sortie in the Mig-21 trainer with Gp. Capt. Sukumar, the CTP. I looped and rolled the aircraft with gay abandon and enjoyed my last ride in a high performance jet. After we landed and parked in the dispersal, I got out and patted the nose of the aircraft—it was like saying goodbye to an old and trusted friend. It was my 3261st sortie on the Mig-21.

Dr C.G.K. Nair was due to demit office as Chairman HAL at the end of August 2001. ACM Tipnis invited both of us for a farewell dinner at Air House in Delhi on 23 August 2001. I went to Delhi with Sheila. A number of senior officers from Air HQ, bureaucrats from the MOD and their wives were present. In his after-dinner speech the CAS spoke about the contributions the two of us had made to aeronautics in general and the LCA programme in particular. In my reply I told the audience that the LCA programme was in exactly the same position the Swedish Gripen programme was 10 years ago and if the Swedes were able to induct the aircraft into Swedish Air Force service by the end of that decade we should be able to do the same with the LCA by 2010.

31 August 2001 dawned bright and clear; it was my last day in IAF service—a little over four enjoyable decades had flashed by since I had entered the august portals of the Air Force Flying College, Jodhpur on 1 July 1961. I had joined the IAF to fly and had flown to my hearts content. 5200 hours flying 75 different types of aircraft, 12 years in fighter squadrons including a spell of operations during the Indo-Pak war in September 1965, 20 years of test flying and I was leaving with nary a scratch on me! I was truly grateful to my guardian angels!

In the afternoon I attended farewell functions at NFTC, HAL (AR&DC) and ASTE. At 5 p.m. when I rose from my chair to leave the office in uniform for the last time the telephone rang. It was Dr K.G. Narayanan who had moved to DRDO Headquarters in Delhi. He said 'Congratulations, your file has been signed by the PM, Atal Behari Vajpayee, promoting you to AOC-in-C's grade from 1 September 2000. Please ring up Yogendra Narain, the Defence Secretary, and thank him'. I promptly rang up Mr. Narain. He said 'All of us were feeling bad that you were being unjustly denied a promotion for no fault of yours and so we invoked a rule by which the PM can authorize a promotion in exceptional circumstances and have the procedures sorted out later. Congratulations'. I thanked him profusely. It felt good to know the MOD had been on my side.

My faith in the system having been so unexpectedly vindicated, I treated my narrow escape from supersession as just reward for my labours in the LCA programme and retired from the IAF a very happy man!

CHAPTER 12

Delay in the First Flight of TD-2 and Negotiations with Foreign Companies

On 1 September 2001, I was back at work at NFTC in civvies, as Dr Aatre had told me to stay on at NFTC till Dr Kota left ADA. This arrangement suited me fine as the IAF had not posted in a replacement for me after my retirement. Dr Kota asked me to lead a team to a Russian agency to hold discussions on the integration of a new CCM on the LCA. The agency was a famous design bureau, the very mention of which sent shivers up the spine of NATO Air Forces during the Cold War because it had developed a string of air-to-air missiles whose capabilities were not known in the West. One of its missiles was specified by the IAF in the weapon list for the LCA. I was of the view that we should get the Original Equipment Manufacturer (OEM) to help us, as no one at ADA or HAL had any experience in doing this type of complex weapon integration.

HAL now had a new Chairman, N.R. Mohanty. He had spent most of his career at HAL Koraput and HAL Nashik and was the Managing Director (Mig Complex), before being appointed Chairman. He had a lot of experience in dealing with recalcitrant labour unions at Koraput and Nashik. He was also well known as a no nonsense taskmaster and a man of utmost rectitude. Fortunately both Dr Kota and I knew Mohanty very well and expected the LCA programme to get his whole-hearted support.

Just as the ADA team was getting ready to leave for Moscow the diabolically-planned and brilliantly executed attack on the twin towers of the World Trade Center in New York took place on 11 September 2001. Within days the US government lifted the sanctions imposed after the Pokharan blasts of May 1998. We at ADA heaved a sigh of relief as we would now get a little more time to allow indigenization plans to fructify.

We left for Moscow a week after the attack for exploratory discussions with the Russians. Having dealt with the Soviet bureaucracy during the Cold War and with Russian organizations after the collapse of the Soviet Union, I expected attitudes regarding customer relations to have changed. I was badly mistaken because the designers refused to accede to any of our requests to adapt their missile integration methods to our avionics architecture. They insisted that the all important missile aircraft interface would be a black box whose innards would be opaque to us. We said we would give them whatever information the carrier aircraft had to provide the missile, in whatever format it was required in. They refused to tell us what information the missile required to function properly! Beyond a point it was not worth arguing with them. Two exhausting weeks later we left after inviting the Russian team to visit ADA in November 2001 to hold further discussions.

The work on TD-2 was going very slowly and there was no hope of flying it in 2001 as planned. TD-2 had been fitted with the indigenous HUD which had been duly certified by CEMILAC. NFTC pilots had worked closely with CSIO, ADE and CEMILAC personnel during the development of the display symbology and the certification process.

There was also a problem of manning at NFTC as Wg. Cdrs. Kothiyal and Nambiar were nearing the end of their period of deputation to ADA. Kothiyal was keen on pursuing a career in civil aviation and did not want to stay in the programme for more than 18 months even if absorbed in ADA as he was already past 43 years of age. He had rendered yeoman service to the programme for six long years and had flown the riskiest first six flights. He had done his fair share. So I let him go back to the IAF to apply for his release from service.

Nambiar was a career officer and was due to command a fighter squadron. I wanted him to do at least a few flights on TD-2 before going back to the IAF, so I asked for a six-month extension of his deputation. The personnel branch at Air HQ insisted that he had to complete his career appointments in time, if he did not want his chances of promotion to the rank of Group Captain to be adversely affected. Change of pilots so early in the programme does not happen in the aircraft industry anywhere in the world. The personnel branch remained in blithe ignorance of the overriding need for continuity in a prototype programme. They seemed oblivious of the fact that flight safety could be adversely affected by a change of pilots after only 12 flights had been flown. Since pilots are frequently posted across squadrons operating different types of aircraft, they must have felt, changeover of pilots at NFTC should also pose no great problem. As I did not want to harm the career of an outstanding officer and test pilot I reluctantly agreed to let Nambiar go though I knew the burden of flight safety on my shoulders would significantly increase. Nambiar was awarded a Bar to his Vayu Sena Medal for the excellent work he did in the programme.

I interviewed two new test pilots, Wg. Cdr. Rakesh Bhaduria and Sqn. Ldr. Suneet Krishna. Bhaduria was an experienced test pilot with mainly Jaguar flying experience while Krishna was from Mig-27s. Both were highly motivated by the professional challenge of participating in a prototype development programme which was half the battle won because a deep sense of commitment was a *sine qua non* for experimental test flying. I requested Air HQ to depute them to ADA. When they reported to NFTC, I told them to get familiar with aircraft systems and start flying the RTS as soon as possible, under the guidance of Banerjee who without flying a single sortie on TD-1, had become the most experienced pilot in the programme! I was determined to ensure that, even with three pilots who had never flown the aircraft before, flight safety should not be compromised.

In November 2001, the Russian team came down and spent

a week at ADA for more discussions on the missile integration project. We made some headway, but the Russians were still loath to part with essential information. We agreed to continue talks in Moscow in January 2002.

In December 2001, TD-2 was readied for its first EGR. A host of problems surfaced and there was no hope of getting it off the ground in a hurry. The biggest problem was blockage of the fuel cooled oil coolers (FCOCs).The aircraft had two FCOCs to cool the hydraulic fluid in both the on board systems, as well as the oil of the 30/40 KVA alternator, and the AMAGB. The fuel carried in the aircraft was to act as the heat sink, and cool the fluids by about 7-8 °C. Unfortunately the sealing compound used to seal the wing fuel tanks started to shed coarse pieces of the compound which went and clogged the inlet to the FCOCs. This was because the wings had been built more than two years ago and fuel had not been filled in the tanks. The blockage reduced the fuel flow in the FCOCs and hence the fluids did not cool to the extent required. After about 30 minutes of the EGR the top temperature limits laid down for safe functioning of the systems were being reached. Numerous cycles of flushing the tanks did not improve matters. We had to finally install a special bowl fuel filter in the inlet line to the FCOCs to resolve the problem. The final solution, of course, was to keep the wing fuel tanks filled with fuel as soon as possible after manufacture. The designers took steps to prevent a recurrence of the problem in the next aircraft.

Towards the end of January 2002, I led an ADA team to Moscow for another round of discussions with the Russians. Moscow was bitterly cold at this time of the year. Day temperatures were in the region of -20 °C. The standard Russian remedy of 100 grams of neat vodka gulped down in one go, immediately after coming indoors from the cold worked very well! This time our technical differences narrowed down quite a bit, and I became hopeful of closing the deal with one more visit to Moscow later that year. I asked them to send us their commercial proposal.

Once the cooling problem was resolved we did a few more

EGRs and started low speed taxi tests in February 2002. When the aircraft started taxiing, a series of hydraulic leaks occurred. Inspectors said the hydraulic plumbing had to be redone. This took a couple of months more. In early April 2002 I handed over the NFTC to Air Commodore A.K. Nagalia who had just relinquished command of ASTE. He became familiar with the aircraft in quick time as I wanted to use the series of EGRs and taxy runs on TD-2 to get him used to the telemetry monitoring function.

We started high speed taxi runs after the FRRB, which I had chaired, and cleared the aircraft for flight in May 2002. Wg. Cdr. Tarun Banerjee was the test pilot selected for the first flight of TD-2. We decided to adopt the same approach we had taken for the first flight of TD-1. This meant asking Air HQ for a Mirage 2000 for chase duties. The military standoff between India and Pakistan after the attack on Parliament on 13 December 2003 was going on and all operational IAF aircraft were committed to various tasks. I spoke to the CAS, ACM Krishnaswamy for a chase Mirage 2000, and he readily agreed to position one at Bangalore for two days. TD-2 did its maiden flight on 6 June 2002. Dr Aatre, N.R. Mohanty and a number of dignitaries were present at the airfield, and I was in my usual position at the telemetry monitoring console!

In retrospect, I think grounding TD-1 after only 12 flights was a big mistake. We had only these flights logged till TD-2 flew a year after we grounded TD-1. We should have continued to fly TD-1 and reached at least the 50 flight milestone. The programme lost much of its momentum. The workforce broke up with key players seeking greener pastures in the private sector.

We had hoped to get TD-2 airborne by September 2001 and simultaneously modify TD-1 to get it back in the air by the end of 2001. Unfortunately the workforce at HAL (AR&DC) was split between the LCA and IJT projects. TD-1 spent the better part of a year standing in a corner of the prototype hangar with its innards stripped. My repeated requests to Dr Aatre to have the Secretary, Defence Production and Supplies (DP&S), under whose charge HAL functioned, exert pressure on HAL to force the pace, had no effect. Dr Aatre could not develop a good equation with the Secretary (DP&S) because of frequent changes of incumbents. The IAF was hesitant to get involved in project management till the technology demonstration phase was over.

In order to keep the programme on the fast track, Dr Kota was able to convince Dr Aatre that a Limited Series Production (LSP) order for some LCA fighters should be placed on HAL. Dr Aatre in turn was able to push the proposal through the finance mandarins at MOD, because the money would come out of the Defence R&D budget. This order was placed on HAL in early June 2002. The management immediately started setting up an assembly line in the aircraft factory. I would have been far happier if the flight test programme of the TDs had been accelerated! This was done before TD-2 flew and we now had to negotiate with US firms for more FCS actuators and GE F404 engines.

Immediately after TD-2 flew, Dr Kota left ADA and went to the Indian Institute of Science to join the faculty. I was now the head of ADA but the person responsible for day-to-day running of the programme was M.B. Verma who had previously been the Project Director in charge of General Systems development. He was an experienced mechanical engineer and had worked in the LCA programme since its inception in 1986.

I now turned my attention to the fresh order for F 404 engines. GE had developed a more advanced version of the F 404 for the South Korean T-50 trainer. It had a much higher Mean Time Between Overhaul (MTBO) than the one we were using and had a Full Authority Digital Engine Control (FADEC). They offered a variant of this engine for the LCA.

In July 2002, I went with a team of ADA, HAL and CEMILAC officers to GE, Lynn, Massachusetts, USA to hold technical negotiations concerning the new variant of the F 404. Dr K.V.L. Rao Project Director (Propulsion) at ADA spearheaded the technical discussions. B.D. Singh, the

Financial Advisor to DG ADA came with us for preliminary discussions on the price of the engine. We spent an absorbing fortnight listening to presentations, holding technical negotiations and meeting GE engineers who were involved in the development of the variant. They told us the development schedule and promised delivery of the first engine in mid-2006. We were convinced that the engine was technically sound and discovered that it produced more thrust and had a higher MTBO, because of new technology single crystal turbine blades. In spite of an increase in the Turbine Inlet Temperature (TIT), these new technology blades had a higher life! We also decided to go for the twin channel FADEC without any hydro-mechanical back-up. We requested GE to send a commercial proposal for the engines and spares.

An interesting feature of the GE team was that many of them were domiciled citizens of the USA. First, there was my old friend Nagui Zakak from Lebanon who was the team leader. He was ably assisted by Mr Gopalan originally from India, Li Teng and Jerry Chu who were Chinese. Li was born in Beijing but his parents had come over to the USA when he was a small boy. Jerry was born in the USA. Nagui went out of his way to look after us. Thanks to him we had our first taste of a Maine lobster dinner washed down with white wine! Another GE engineer Tony Chamay had a power boat and we spent a lovely Saturday afternoon cruising up and down the Massachusetts coastline, weaving this way and that, to avoid the innumerable brightly-coloured lobster pot buoys which dotted the surface of the sea.

On our return we told Dr Aatre that approval to go ahead with purchase of the engines should be pushed through the MOD in Delhi as soon as possible. These engines would meet the requirements of the prototype development programme up to FOC, the limited series production order and the Naval LCA prototypes. The delivery schedule promised by GE fitted in nicely with our plans.

The FCS of the LCA used high performance hydraulic actuators designed by Lockheed Martin, Flight Control Division, at Binghampton, New York. This was known as Martin Marrieta Control Systems (MMCS) before it was acquired by Lockheed Martin. These actuators were manufactured by a company called Moog at Buffalo, New York. When an agreement was signed by ADE with MMCS way back in 1992, it was agreed by both parties, that all procurement of hardware for the FCS would be done only by MMCS. The Indian side represented by ADE could not place orders directly with any vendor like Moog. Very few sets of actuators were procured initially for the technology demonstration phase, because no one was confident that the fly-by-wire FCS would be successfully developed, and the finance department would allow only the bare minimum expenditure. Of these sets some were instrumented internally for flight test purposes. This parsimonious approach caused the development team any number of headaches. One full set of actuators was required for use on the Iron Bird and a half set was required on the mini-bird at ADE! Qualification testing took up another set. This left us with barely enough sets for the two flying aircraft and any unserviceability of the actuators such as high internal leak rates had to be attended to, only at the manufacturer's facility, and that too after the hardware had been routed through Lockheed Martin. Even this unsatisfactory system enabled us to continue development work albeit with frequent hold ups due to lack of actuators or sensor hardware which had developed faults.

After imposition of sanctions post-Pokharan in May 1998, life was positively harrowing! There was simply no way open to us to get faulty hardware rectified and put back into use. Very fortunately for us the Moog actuators had been manufactured to extremely high quality standards and did not suffer from any major failures. We were constantly switching actuators from the aircraft to the Iron bird, and vice versa. We requested the CEMILAC and DGAQA inspectors to adopt a practical rather than a bookish approach to clearing supposedly faulty actuators, which were marginally outside specifications for use on the ground. When we finally flew

TD-1 we had little more than one fully serviceable set of actuators which was on the aircraft!

Early in 1998 an ADA/ADE team had gone to Binghampton and negotiated for the supply of more sets of actuators, but Lockheed Martin did not take any action to execute the order because of the sanctions. Our first priority now was to revive the order. When we started talking to Lockheed Martin we were told that there had been a steep escalation in costs due to the delay caused by the sanctions. Our plea that we had not cancelled the order, and that the sanctions had been imposed by the US government and not India, had no effect! We had to negotiate a new price and delivery schedule with them.

In August 2002, I headed for Binghampton, New York this time with a team of FCS specialists from ADE and ADA. As ADE was the DRDO laboratory responsible for development of the FCS and had been working closely with Lockheed Martin Flight Controls Division, Aruvamudam, Director ADE, led the talks. I made a special request to Dr Aatre to include Dr K.G. Narayanan, who had retired, in the team, as he was well known to Lockheed Martin. Both Aruvamudam and I were visiting Binghampton for the first time and it made good sense to have someone who knew the other side well. Dr Aatre was able to get special GOI sanction for the inclusion of Dr K.G. Narayanan in the team. The talks went well and we signed a fresh contract for the delivery of the actuators ordered in 1998, with the first set to be delivered in July 2004. For good measure, we included an option for more sets in the contract which would take care of the LSP order of aircraft also.

Tarun Banerjee flew the first six flights on TD-2 and after that both Rakesh Bhaduria and Suneet 'Soggy' Krishna started to fly the aircraft. Air HQ then posted Tarun out to take over command of a upgraded Mig Bison unit. I was again faced with the problem of relatively inexperienced pilots flying the two TDs. By now, however, NFTC had evolved a proper training syllabus for new test pilots entering the programme and thanks to the excellent fidelity of the RTS, flight safety was never compromised.

I recommended Tarun Banerjee for a Vayu Sena Medal for his contribution to the programme. I was delighted to see his name in the Republic Day awards list on 26 January 2003.

In September 2002 I had to go to Moscow to close the deal for CCM integration on the LCA. Before going there I called on ACM Krishnaswamy at Air HQ and brought him up to date with the progress made in development of the MMR. I told him that while progress was heartening, it would not be ready for weapon integration work to start some time in early 2005. I said a decision had to be taken soon on the radar to be fitted in the LCA for the IOC phase. I suggested that the IAF should look closely at three candidate radars which were available in the world market, and take a quick decision to enable ADA to start the long process of negotiations with vendors. Once the radar was identified there was a substantial amount of structural and avionics integration work to be done, and time was of the essence. The CAS said he would like a radar already in use in the IAF to be fitted in the LCA also. He felt the IAF could not afford to have a large number of different radars in its inventory and a commonality of radars between some of the existing fleet and the LCA was highly desirable. While the CAS certainly had a point, I did not agree with this view as it would take some more years for the LCA to enter service, and it would thereafter remain in use for at least four decades. I wanted the LCA to enter service with a state-of-the-art radar with adequate potential for growth as new technology became available. I decided to send my views in writing to Air HQ on my return from Russia.

In Moscow we ran into an unexpected problem. The company was not authorized by the Russian Government to conduct commercial negotiations without the involvement of the official government agency in charge of all arms exports, Rosoboronexport. At the last minute, when we were about to finalize the contract, the Rosoboronexport officials demanded a huge increase in price and I was forced to break off the negotiations and return home empty-handed. I was bitterly disappointed at this failure which I was sure would lead to a delay in the grant of IOC to the aircraft. We had to look for other partners to complete the task which meant starting negotiations all over again. The only saving grace during our stay in Moscow was a visit to the Bolshoi theatre to see the ballet *Giselle* performed by the world renowned Bolshoi Ballet troupe. It was a divine experience.

In October 2002, NFTC had a new head, Air Commodore Parvez Khokhar, an experienced test pilot and a former Commandant ASTE. Air Commodore Nagalia had moved on promotion as ACAS (Plans), at Air HQ. Nagalia, in the six months he had spent at NFTC, had applied himself with his customary zeal to the task at hand and had a good grasp of the many hurdles that had to be crossed before IOC of the aircraft could be achieved. I felt it was good to have someone who was fully conversant with the programme, at the decision making level at Air Hq. The LCA needed friends in high places!

TD-2 continued to notch up test flights at a rate of about 4-5 flights per month but no significant progress could be made in expanding the flight envelope because it was flying with the same fixed gain CLAW we had used in the first block of flights for TD-1. To start expanding the envelope, we needed to get TD-1 back in the air with the scheduled gain CLAW. For this the LES and the air brakes had to be made functional, and the fuel system had to be modified, to allow full internal fuel to be used in the air. The CLAW team had developed the required CLAW and offered it for HQ evaluation at the RTS to NFTC pilots who were happy with it. The CLAW was now being integrated in the DFCC and had to go to the Iron Bird for validation and pilot in loop checks.

A third test pilot, Wg. Cdr. Vikram Singh joined NFTC in December 2002. He had considerable experience on the Mirage 2000 and was a very welcome addition to the team.

The division of the workforce between HAL's IJT programme and the LCA programme continued to take its toll. In the second half of 2002, HAL decided to make an all-out effort to get the IJT into the air before AeroIndia 2003, scheduled to be held in the second week of February 2003. HAL management even thought of making the IJT fly at the air show in much the same way as the LCA had done at AeroIndia 2001. During my frequent visits to the AR&DC hangar I had seen the prototype being worked upon by a crowd of technicians and the rapid progress that was being made in manufacturing the prototype. In spite of this and the fact that the IJT was an aircraft equipped with manual flight controls which did not need years of development time, I was certain that it could not be flown before the air show.

I was of the view that having displayed one LCA at the previous air show, this time we should aim to show both TD-1 and TD-2 flying in formation at the opening ceremony, in front of the Raksha Mantri and the international aviation community. Later, one of the aircraft could take part in the daily flying display, while the other could be on static display with an array of weapons laid out in front of it. For this to happen TD-1 had to fly by the last week of December 2002, to give NFTC pilots enough time to practise formation flying and participate in the fly past rehearsals.

Late one evening in early December 2002 I went to the prototype flight hangar on my way home. I found the two LCAs standing forlornly in the hangar with not a soul in sight. TD-1 was in a stripped down state and I could see that considerable work remained to be done before we could think of EGRs, taxi tests and flight. I called Dr Aatre and told him to speak to the Secretary, Defence Production and Supplies to request HAL to pay adequate attention to the LCA project as well. The next day I got a message that Mohanty was visiting the prototype hangar and would like to see me. I went to the hangar and told Mohanty of ADA's plan to fly both the LCAs at AeroIndia 2003. He promised all help.

There was considerable improvement in the pace of work, but we had fallen too far behind the schedule required to make an impressive appearance at AeroIndia 2003. We tried our best to force the pace without compromising safety but to no avail. By the time we did the first EGR it was 20 January 2003. The new CLAW had been cleared on the Iron Bird and

I was still hoping to do about four test flights with the scheduled gain CLAW before the opening day of the air show, 5 February 2003. Unfortunately, we ran into a serious problem with the scheduled gain CLAW. During the first high speed taxi test on 30 January 2003, when Gp. Capt. Bhaduria went past 220 kmph on the runway the elevons started to flap violently causing the aircraft to bounce up and down like a bucking bronco! Bhaduria managed to control it in time by throttling back the engine and reducing speed. Everyone was a bit shaken.

The flight test data showed that the problem had been caused by the 'soft' suspension of the nose wheel. As the aircraft went over undulations in the runway the nose wheel bobbed up and down much like a car wheel going over a bumpy road. This bumpy motion was picked up by the fly-by-wire FCS which made the elevons flap! I was relieved because we were able to pinpoint the exact cause of the problem. As re-design of the nose wheel suspension would take considerable time, we decided to take-off and land in fixed gains as the elevons would not flap in this mode and select the new CLAW only in the air till the nose wheel with the new suspension arrived.

At 1700 hrs on 3 February 2003, TD-1 finally took to the air after spending 20 months on the ground. This compared very favourably with the 18 months the Eurofighter Typhoon spent on the ground after its first block of 20 flights. The test flight went well and the scheduled gain CLAW was trouble-free. There was no time to recover the aircraft at Bangalore and position it at Yelahanka the next day for the static display on 5 February 2003. I told Ravi at the telemetry monitoring console to tell Bhaduria to land at Yelahanka itself. He managed to land a few minutes before last daylight landing time and a complete loss of face for ADA was prevented. We would now have one aircraft participating in the flying display and one would be on static display. It was not as good a situation as displaying both aircraft in formation on the opening day, but it was not a disaster either. Of course, the IJT was still about a month away from its maiden flight. My prediction made to Dr Aatre a few months earlier that we would neither be able to display two LCAs in the air nor the IJT at AeroIndia 2003 came true.

At the end of the opening ceremony of Aero India 2003 on 5 February 2003, there was a flypast of IAF aircraft. TD-2 flown by Soggy Krishna did a high speed run followed by a zoom climb and a wing over which took it out of sight. We had only the fixed gain CLAW on TD-2 and poor Soggy had to execute his manoeuvres very gingerly to avoid exceeding limits. After the flypast was over all the invitees repaired to a big marquee for high tea, following which the NFTC pilots and I walked down to TD-1 on static display in the hope the RM, George Fernandes, would come to see the aircraft with all the external stores and weapons laid out in front of it. While we waited in eager anticipation the RM and the CAS drove past TD-1 straight to the HAL stall. I found out later that the RM was being shown the mock up of the Light Attack Helicopter (LAH) which had been projected as an IAF requirement. TD-2 flew without incident on all five days of the show much to the relief of all at ADA and HAL. The flight test programme crossed the 50 flight milestone during the show.

CHAPTER 13

Flutter, the Naming Ceremony, Supersonic Flight and Retirement

When the dust settled down after Aero India 2003, we started expanding the flight envelope on TD-1. To do that our engineers from the aero structures group came out with a flutter test plan.

Let me first explain what flutter is. Since an aircraft has to fly, it has to have a lightweight structure. The need to keep an aircraft structure light results in reduced stiffness. An aircraft's wing is therefore flexible and can easily bend and twist under the influence of air loads. Under certain conditions of flight, dynamic air loads begin to increase the flexible motion of the wing which further increases the air loads. The increased air loads may eventually exceed the structural strength of the wing causing it to break. Such a catastrophic dynamic coupling between elastic motion and air loads is called flutter. What makes the phenomenon particularly dangerous is its sudden onset. Everything may be normal up to a particular speed, and flutter may occur 1 kmph later. Such events are called 'cliff edges' in flight test parlance and have to be approached with extreme caution.

The method of carrying out flutter testing in a fly-by-wire aircraft is to excite airframe frequencies at various height/speed combinations using the FCS actuators. The FCS group at ADE had developed a Flight Test Panel (FTP) in which 100 pre-determined inputs of various frequencies and amplitudes could be programmed before a test sortie, and injected directly to the actuator bypassing the DFCC. This meant all the safety features in the DFCC and FCS failure warnings were not available during flutter testing. We had to devise new ways of ensuring flight safety and this required a lot of brain storming. The aircraft would have to be specially instrumented, and important information concerning flight safety telemetered down to the monitoring station. A team from the aerostructures group would have to sit at the monitors and analyse the data in a very short while (1-2 minutes) and if satisfied, clear the pilot to proceed to the next test point. This way productivity and safety of flutter test flights would improve quite significantly. All this was being done in the advanced nations for some years, but we would be doing it for the first time.

The software for excitation inputs from the FTP had to be developed, verified and validated with the same rigour with which all the FCS software had been developed. We integrated the FTP in the Iron Bird and checked out each of the 100 frequencies and all the safety features built into the FTP. Wg. Cdr. B.B. Misra of the CLAW team played a major role in developing the functionality of the FTP.

The aerostructures group at ADA had developed an analytical flutter model of the aircraft in their computer. The model showed that the basic airframe was flutter free throughout the proposed flight envelope. In addition, a delta wing is structurally stiff because of its big wing root chord. I was of the view that we would need very few flutter tests till we reached 740 kmph. At a height of about 11 km this speed would correspond to Mach 1. I based my view on the fact that the dynamic pressure at that speed was only 25 kilo pascals and the analytical model showed the airframe was flutter free up to a dynamic pressure of 85 kilo pascals (1 pascal is the pressure exerted by a force of 1 Newton on an area of 1 sq metre). The aerostructures group, however, insisted that the transonic region between Mach 0.9 and Mach 1.1 was their area of greatest concern, as they did not want to take a chance with the effect of shock waves on the airframe. Beyond a point I could not argue with the designers, because it was their responsibility and we had to wait for the green light to go supersonic from them. To go supersonic the speed envelope had to be expanded from 610 kmph to 740 kmph.

The IJT prototype was to do its first flight on 7 March 2003 with Sqn. Ldr. (Retd) Baldev Singh at the controls. I went and wished him a safe flight before he started the engine. Due to the tremendous effort put in by HAL AR&DC the aircraft flew just 22 months after the first cutting of metal. I was with Mohanty by the side of the runway when the aircraft took off and congratulated him and the entire HAL team present there.

Dr Aatre now told us that the Prime Minister Atal Behari Vajpayee had expressed a desire to see the LCA. We wanted to give an Indian name to the aircraft and thought it would be an excellent idea if we could have the aircraft named by the PM himself. This was agreed to by the PMO and 4 May 2003 was fixed as the day for the PM's visit. For good measure we heard that the Deputy PM L.K. Advani would also accompany the PM.

Thanks to the ever-present threat from terrorist elements in our society, a VVIP visit is a nightmare for the organizers! As the venue for the event was the Bangalore airport which belonged to HAL, we did not have to worry about security as it would be taken care of by HAL security personnel. Teams from the PM's security staff started arriving well before the date to check out the arrangements. Every little detail had to be attended to and the expected movements of the PM were mapped and timed. The invitee list was also scrutinized and approved by the PMO.

A list of a dozen Sanskrit names was forwarded to the PMO and we were not told of the PM's choice till the very end! Chairman HAL wanted to use the PM's visit to HAL to display the Intermediate Jet Trainer and the Advanced Light Helicopter (ALH) also. The total time allotted for the flying display was 10 minutes!

At ADA our job was to ensure that an impressive flying display was put up by the two TDs. Air Cmde. Parvez Khokhar did an excellent job of organizing the display which was to last precisely three minutes! We had a small problem in flying two LCA TDs in formation, as TD-1 was flying with scheduled gains, while TD-2 still had the old fixed gains. Bhaduria and Krishna practised formation flying with Krishna in TD-2 in the lead and Bhaduria in TD-1 carrying out formation on him. Khokhar then asked the two pilots whether they were comfortable enough to attempt a formation take off! Both agreed with alacrity! I was called to see the first practice formation take-off and I must admit I had butterflies in my stomach! Since the aircraft were behaving well and the pilots were confident I did not say anything. The formation take-off was spectacular.

Having lost an opportunity to show off two LCAs in the air at Aero India 2003 I thought it would be a good idea to do so now, with a bang. Since we had been given only three minutes to display the capabilities of the LCA we had to do something special! The electronic and print media would splash it all over the country and abroad. I approved the proposal to do a formation take-off in front of the PM and Deputy PM. Everyone thought I was sticking my neck out on a limb but in my mind I knew the risk was quite acceptable.

HAL had spared no effort to make arrangements for the PM's visit. It was decided that along with the PM and Deputy PM, the RM George Fernandes, the CAS ACM Krishnaswamy, Chairman HAL Mohanty, and Dr Aatre would sit on a special dais set-up to one side of the Bangalore runway. The spot was chosen so that the dignitaries had a clear view of the full length of the runway in use. Other VIPs, HAL and ADA personnel and invitees were seated in a separate enclosure, a bit removed from the main dais. This was another requirement put forward by the PM's security staff. We positioned LCA PV-1, which had been fully equipped, on static display behind the dais.

4 May 2003 turned out to be a lovely day with bright sunshine and a cloudless sky. The two LCAs taxied out and lined up for take-off on the active runway before the PM arrived. At exactly 1000 hours the PM arrived and took his place on

the dais. As he sat down the two aircraft roared down the runway and lifted off in front of the dais in impeccable formation. They went through their pre-planned routine and landed one behind the other after three minutes. It was a most impressive performance even if I say so myself. The TV camera crews had a field day and the LCA programme received wide publicity. Long after the event, Indian TV programmes continued to show two LCAs taking off in formation.

After the IJT and ALH had completed their routines, the speeches started. When the PM spoke he congratulated every one for the progress the country had made in aeronautics in general, and in the LCA programme in particular. He named the LCA, Tejas which means 'radiance' in Sanskrit.

After the speeches the PM went round to meet the test pilots and test engineers of NFTC, all the Project Directors of ADA and the HAL (AR&DC) team. The CAS and Dr Aatre congratulated me for a good show. I was relieved that everything had gone according to plan. The 75 flight milestone was crossed during the display for the PM.

After the PM's visit I had less than four months to go for my two-year tenure as Director ADA to end. I set myself a small goal of reaching 100 flights with three aircrafts in the air by 31 August 2003. I also wanted the aircraft to go supersonic before I left.

We grounded TD-2 to be modified to the same standard as TD-1. Yogesh Kumar, Executive Director, AR&DC at HAL had said he would need three months to carry out the modifications. Yogesh had made a most praiseworthy contribution to the LCA programme in far from ideal circumstances, and I only hoped that he would be able to deliver on his commitment to fly TD-2 some time in August 2003. The check out of PV-1 for flight had to be accelerated, for my dream of three aircraft in the sky at the same time to be realized. I made several visits to the hangar and made personal appeals to the workers to meet the targets I had set. They promised to do their utmost to achieve these goals.

Speed envelope expansion from 610 kmph to 740 kmph

continued on TD-1 all through May, June and July with numerous flutter test points. By the end of July 2003, 740 kmph speed was reached. The altitude envelope had been increased to 12 km and we were all set to go supersonic. On 1 August 2003, Dr Aatre, Mohanty and I assembled in the debriefing room next to the LCA's parking slot. Wg. Cdr. Vikram Singh started up TD-1 at 0930 hours but the chase Mirage 2000 did not! When the Mirage was rectified the weather clamped down! Finally at 1530 hours the weather cleared sufficiently for Vikram to get airborne and make the attempt. We went to the telemetry monitoring room and heard him call out his Mach No. as he accelerated at 11 km. He went to Mach 0.95 and then became silent. This is normal because the pressure instrument readings become unreliable as the shock wave crosses the pressure ports of the aircraft and the pilot has to wait till he has crossed Mach 1 before the instruments read accurately again. We then heard him call out Mach 1.08 and say that the aircraft had behaved perfectly while crossing the sonic barrier. A cheer went up from the three of us. I had expressly forbidden any show of emotion by the engineers at the monitoring consoles lest they miss any abnormal behaviour of the aircraft!

In the last week of August I went to Rashtrapati Bhawan and presented my old boss President Abdul Kalam with a photograph of two LCAs flying in formation. Dr C.G.K. Nair accompanied me. When I told the President I was retiring at the end of the month he said 'Not many people in India have your kind of experience. Why don't you become a teacher and pass on your rich experience of working in a prototype development programme to the younger generation'. I have followed the President's advice and given talks regularly to student test pilots and flight test engineers at the Air Force Test Pilots School at ASTE, Bangalore.

Just a couple of days before I retired, I went to Air HQ on my last official visit to attend the VCAS's bi-monthly review of the LCA programme. Air Marshal M. McMahon was in the chair. At that forum I made a presentation regarding the planning required to carry out proper evaluation of the MMR, the Kaveri engine and the trainer. I said we needed at least two dedicated aircraft for each of these three complex tasks. I suggested a way forward to achieve weapons integration and Initial Operational Clearance (IOC) quickly.

By 31 August 2003, we could complete only 98 flights. I received a nice letter from Dr Aatre thanking me for my contribution to the LCA programme to which I replied and suggested a way forward, which I was convinced was the only way weapons integration could be carried out and Initial Operational Clearance (IOC) achieved quickly. I handed over charge to M.B. Verma and called it a day!

TD-2 had to fly with the scheduled gains CLAW which meant the LES and air brakes had to be made operational. In addition, the fuel system had to be modified to make full internal fuel available to the engine. When the aircraft was flying with fixed gains we were using only partial internal fuel to maintain the CG within limits. I had hoped that the modifications would be completed in three months, but it took close to six months. The aircraft flew in October 2003.

M.B. Verma called me in November 2003 to complete the FRRB for PV-1, the third aircraft, which I had started when I was still at ADA. The FRRB met for its third and final meeting on 10 November 2003, and cleared the aircraft for high speed taxi tests leading to first flight. The aircraft finally flew on 25 November 2003 with 'Soggy' Krishna at the controls.

ADA and HAL went into overdrive in early 2004 and flew no less than 38 flights on the three LCAs in March 2004. The technology demonstration milestones of 202 flights (the aim was to fly between 200–20 flights) and the agreed flight envelope were achieved by 31 March 2004. This marked the end of Phase 1 of the LCA programme. This was only three months later than the earlier projected date of completion of 31 December 2003.

I had greatly enjoyed working in the programme for nine years and retired with a sense of satisfaction. This was because of the successful accomplishment of most of the risky phases of flight testing required for technology demonstration, for which the IAF had sent me on deputation to ADA. A large number of technical and managerial challenges had to be overcome and there never was a dull moment in a day's work. I set-up the NFTC from scratch and introduced a systematic professional approach to flight testing which will stand the programme in good stead in the years ahead. The successful first flight of the aircraft during the height of the US sanctions regime and the completion of a further 97 flights without any mishap were achievements I am proud of. By any yardstick the LCA technology demonstration programme was fraught with many risks because of the several new technologies packed into a prototype aircraft and our own inexperience. On top of that I took calculated risks and got away with it. Fortune certainly favoured the brave!

CHAPTER 14

Postscript

The second Tejas prototype vehicle, PV-2, executed its maiden flight on 1 December 2005. I was the Chairman of the FRRB which cleared the aircraft for its first flight. This aircraft was powered by a GE F 404 F2J3 engine like the other three aircraft participating in the flight test programme. It had a production standard airframe, a completely new avionics suite and a development model of the Multi Mode Radar fitted in the nose. Press reports indicated that Initial Operational Clearance (IOC) would be granted by the end of 2008.

The Tejas can be inducted into the IAF inventory in the next decade. Now that the Technology Demonstration phase has been successfully completed the project must be gradually brought under a single agency, which should be the industry. The IAF must be responsible for programme management. ADA must transfer the fly-by-wire FCS, composite airframe and glass cockpit technologies to HAL, and concentrate on the design of the naval and trainer variants. Serious attention must be paid to product support from this stage onwards, or else the IAF will not be able to exploit the aircraft in service.

It is perhaps the right time to ask the question 'Will the emerging global role of the IAF in the next 25 years require an aircraft of the Tejas class in its inventory? For almost four decades when India had adopted a defensive posture, and defending national airspace was considered of prime importance, the backbone of the IAF's fighter fleet was the Russian Mig-21. The short range and small weapon load of the Mig-21 did not render it unsuitable for the air defence role because the IAF had developed a chain of forward airbases from Thoise in Ladakh to Naliya on the Western seaboard of Gujarat. Similarly in the North-East airfields stretched from Bagdogra in North Bengal to Tezu in Arunachal Pradesh. The threat was assumed to be from our western and northern neighbours only. When IAF planners started to look around for a replacement for the Mig-21 in the early 1980s the defensive orientation of the force was expected to continue into the foreseeable future. They felt that any replacement should have contemporary technology but did not want a big aircraft, as costs tends to rise dramatically with weight. Affordability was a key driver for the planners. A single engine multi-role fighter with slightly greater payload and range than the Mig-21 was asked for.

During the long gestation period of the project the global geo-strategic scene has changed beyond the wildest imagination of IAF planners of the 1980s. The collapse of the Soviet Union, the emergence of a sole Super Power, the spread of global terrorism, the failure or break-up of a number of states like Somalia, Afghanistan and Yugoslavia, reduced tension with Pakistan and China, the need for energy to fuel the rapid economic growth of India following liberalization all call for a reorientation of national defence policy. This is a political decision which merits serious attention of the elected representatives of the people in Parliament and clearly beyond the scope of my narrative.

The Tejas has been developed to requirements laid down in the mid-1980s. Thanks to the foresight of IAF planners and the untiring efforts of ADA/DRDO/HAL/IAF, the aircraft has the technology and performance to perform a useful role for the IAF for the next two decades. After that a mid-life upgrade should be able to extend its life further. The reason for my confidence in the future usefulness of the aircraft stems from the fact that it has some capabilities which make it comparable to its peers in other air forces of the world. These are, a MMR which will confer Beyond Visual Range (BVR) missile launch capability, a Helmet Mounted Display (HMD) which will give look and shoot CCM launch capability, a fourth generation avionics suite with up to date man-machine interface in the cockpit, secure communication equipment, data link, a state of the art Electronic Warfare (EW) suite and extended range and loiter capability with aerial refuelling. In BVR engagements the maximum range of the missile will be of crucial importance, and the Tejas will need to be always equipped with the best missile in that class. The aircraft will also have significant air-to-ground capability by both day and night. It must, however, be understood that it is a relatively small aircraft and cannot match the agility, power, range and payload of a Sukhoi 30 MKI or a F-22 Raptor, both of which are much more expensive aircrafts. Intelligent choice of its theatre of operations will be required. Maintainability and reliability data of the aircraft and its MMR can only be gathered after IOC has been declared, but every effort is being made by the developing agencies to ensure that IAF requirements in this regard will be met.

Finally, I must answer the big question—Was the LCA project successful, and how far have the three original aims of the project, which were bridging the technology gap in aeronautics, indigenization and delivery of a ready-to-go to war machine to the IAF at a reasonable cost and time-frame, been achieved. The technology gap has certainly been bridged in that our scientists and engineers can design a digital fly-by-wire FCS, a glass cockpit and a composite airframe from scratch for any aircraft. Manufacturing technology has been upgraded and indigenization of a large number of critical components has been achieved leading to spin offs in several areas. The speed with which the IJT took to the air from inception of the project was impressive. It took only 22 months from go-ahead to first flight. This would not have been possible but for the capabilities developed for the LCA project. A number of foreign aerospace companies gave invaluable support at the development stage, but we have absorbed the relevant technologies.

We must, however, have the courage to admit that in certain areas we have not succeeded to the desired extent. The Kaveri engine which was to power the LCA is not likely to be certified for some more time. India cannot call itself an aerospace player of any significance until we succeed in developing our own jet engine. Though the MMR has come a long way and the portents for successful development of this primary sensor are good it would be naïve to pretend that it has been successfully developed. There is some time and distance to go yet.

The good news is that cost of the LCA project as a whole has been well controlled and the final bill will be far less than the cost of a similar project anywhere in the developed world. Unlike some civilian infrastructure projects where large scale 'leakage' of funds takes place, the LCA project has been scam-free since its inception.

In order to build on these gains it will be necessary to start another combat aircraft development project in the next few years, before the skill sets developed in the workforce evaporate. India must insist on a significant share of design work in any fifth generation fighter development project if it decides to join hands with a foreign aerospace major. For this new project it will be good if the time-tested model of aeronautical development followed in the Western world is adopted. In that environment, new technologies are developed by the R&D agencies, the aeronautical industry designs and develops the aircraft and the uniformed user service manages the project. Ad hoc programme management offices should not be created.

My 42 years in aviation were absorbing and deeply rewarding. I joined the IAF to fly fast jets. It was a boyhood dream which turned into a man's profession. I first learned to fly, then to fight in the air, then to test aircraft and finally got involved in the design and development of a fourth generation fighter. The journey gave me a ringside seat to view the breathtaking pace of technological change in aeronautics, which turned out to be a humbling experience. The more one tried to learn and catch up with technology, the more it became apparent that one knew so little. I was reminded of Isaac Newton's statement that he was like a small boy playing on the seashore finding a shiny pebble here and there while the vast ocean of knowledge lay unexplored before him. I will end my narrative by saying that the great scientist was dead right, as in the final analysis one does not learn too much in a lifetime.

Index

Aatre, V.K. 19, 113, 116, 120, 125, 137, 140, 144, 146, 156–60
Above Ground Level (AGL) 49
Active Matrix Liquid Crystal Displays (AMLCDs) 77
ADA MOU with HAL 35–6
Advanced Light Helicopter (ALH) 156
Advanced Systems Integration and Evaluation Organization (ASIEO) 78
Advani, L.K. 156
Aero India 2001 133–4; of 2003 150–1, 157–9
Aeronautical Development Agency (ADA) 15–16, 20, 24–5, 28–41, 62–9, 73–7, 83–107, 116, 118, 132, 137, 140–6, 148–9, 151, 155–7, 160–1
Air Force Flying College, Jodhpur 139
air show *see* Aero India
Air Staff Requirement (ASR) 30
Air Staff Target (AST) 28
Air Traffic Control (ATC) 21–2, 24, 47, 118, 123–4
Airborne Early Warning project 108
Aircraft and Systems Testing Establishment (ASTE) 36
Aircraft Mounted Auxiliary Gear Box (AMAGB) 35, 96–7
Aircraft Research and Design Centre (AR&DC) 84, 103
Ajeet fighter 27–8, 36, 57
Alam, Sqn. Ldr. Anjali 19
Alenia of Italy 16, 34
All Purpose Flying Instructors Course 60
Alliance Air Boeing 737-200 crashed at Patna 119–22; CDR data of 121
Allison, Dave 116
Alpha Jet Advanced Jet Trainer (AJT) 59
AN-32 transport aircraft 59
Antonov test pilot, Katchienko 59
Armament Research and Development Establishment (ARDE) 58
Arunachalam, V.S. 30, 32; for DRDO a world class R&D organization 29; handed over DRDO to Dr A.P.J. Abdul Kalam 34
Aruvamudam, ADE Director 148
ASTE 36–8, 57–61, 63–4, 68, 74–5, 78, 82, 85, 93, 108, 114, 129, 138–9, 144, 150, 159
Ati Vishisht Seva Medal (AVSM) 131
Avro 748 H-2176 58, 60, 93; aircraft crashed 108

BAe Systems (British Aerospace), UK 16, 29–30, 111; consultants Harry Widger and Keith Hulme 92; simulator 88
Ball, John 89
Banerjee, Wg. Cdr. Tarun 144; flew on TD-2 148–9; as Sqn. Ldr. 101, 111, 117, 128; for Vayu Sena Medal 149

Beyond Visual Range (BVR) 93, 163–5
Bhaduria, Gp. Capt. Rakesh 142, 152
brake-by-wire system 109
Brar, Flt. Lt. Darshan Singh 50–3, 114
Brar, Air Marshal Prithvi Singh 114
Brevet de Pilote d'Essais 57

Calspan 76
Canberra trainer 60
CEMILAC and DGAQA 102, 147; certification 124
Central Scientific Instrumentation Organization (CSIO) at Chandigarh 91
Centre for Airborne Systems (CABS) 66–7
C-H scale 82
Chamay, Tony 146
Chandrashekar, Ahalya CEMILAC, 73
Chetty, Shyam 74, 80
Chief Test Pilot (CTP) 36, 57, 61, 78, 101, 125, 138
China war and Pandit Nehru 46
Chu, Jerry 146
cliff edges 154
Close Compact Missile (CCM) 58, 140, 149, 163
Cockpit Evaluation Facility (CEF) 68, 79, 98, 130
Combat Vehicle Research and Development Establishment (CVRDE) 96–7
Computational Fluid Dynamics (CFD) 72
Computer Aided Design (CAD)/ Computer Aided Manufacture (CAM) 84–5
Computer Aided Manufacture (CAM) facilities 85
Control Law (CLAW) 38, 63, 67, 72, 90, 100, 114; designers 81; development of 73–4; engineers 88; wing team formed by Dr Kalam 35
Council for Scientific and Industrial Research (CSIR) 74, 91
Crash Data Recorder (CDR) 120

Darin Jaguar 79
DARIN second generation Nav/ Attack system 58
Dassault Aviation of France 16, 29–30, 32, 45, 101
David, Clement Somasundaram 42
David, Grace Kamala mother 42
De Havilland Vampire 43
Defence Evaluation and Research Agency (DERA) 92–3
Defence Production and Supplies (DP&S), 144–5
Defence Research and Development Organization (DRDO) 29–31, 34–40, 59, 63, 108, 113, 116, 132–3, 139, 148, 163
Dell 133
Deodhare, Girish 74, 80
Devayya, Sqn. Ldr. A.B. 48, 50; awarded posthumous Maha Vir Chakra 54
digital back-up (DBU) system 72, 83, 93
Digital Flight Control Computer (DFCC) 70, 78, 92, 100, 103, 111, 113; software 105, 110; and FCS 154
digital fly-by-wire Flight Control System (FCS) 20–2
digital notch filters were integrated with the CLAW 109
Directorate General of Aeronautical Quality Assurance, The (DGAQA) 124
Directorate of Aeronautical Quality Assurance (DGAQA) 105

Dornier of Germany 29
DRDO laboratory at Bangalore 29–31, 34–40, 59, 63, 108, 113, 116, 132–3, 139, 149, 163
Dynamic Avionics Integration Rig (DAIR) 68, 79, 106, 130

Easter, Russ 89
Ecole du Personnel Navigant d'Essais et de Reception (EPNER) France 21
economy and India 34
Electro Magnetic Compatibility (EMC) 123–4
Electro Magnetic Interference (EMI) 123–4
Electronic Warfare (EW) 163
engine ground run (EGR) 97, 114, 130
Engineer in Loop Simulator (ELS) 75, 99
Environmental Cooling System (ECS) 114–15
Euro fighter programme 117
Earle, Patrick Russel 'Paddy' 46, 48

F-16 CLAW 89
F-22 Raptor programme 136
F-404 engine on TD-1 90; orders for 145
Fernandes, George (Raksha Mantri) 27, 131, 153, 157
Final Operational Clearance (FOC) 58, 73, 146
Flight Control System (FCS) 23, 26, 28, 30–4, 37–8, 61, 65–8, 71–6, 80–1, 84–5, 90–3, 95–6, 99–100, 103–9, 111–17, 127, 130, 133, 145–8, 154–5, 163–4
Flight Control System (FCS) 30–8, 65–8, 71–6, 80–1, 84–5, 95–6, 99; development 90–1; engineers 99; failure warnings 111; hardware 105, 114, software 27
Flight Mechanics and Controls Division (FMCD) 74
Flight Readiness Review Board (FRRB) 113–14
Flight Test Engineers (FTEs) 60
Flight Test Instrumentation Engineer (FTIE) 60, 64
Flight Test Panel (FTP) 154–5
flutter 154
fly-by-wire Flight Control System (FCS) 28, 30, 34, 70, 73, 147; as real time simulator (RTS) 67
Flying Instructors School at Tambaram 60
French; digi-ana hybrid FCS 32
fuel cooled oil coolers (FCOCs) 143
Full Authority Digital Engine Control (FADEC) 145–6
Functionality Requirement Document (FRD) 98, 105

Gandhi, Indira 28
Gandhi, Rajiv 29, 31, 33, 34; assassination of 34
Gas Turbine Research Establishment (GTRE) 96
GE F404 F2J3 15, 21, 31, 45, 95, 120, 133, 162
Glass Cockpit 20, 28, 63, 70, 77–9, 134, 162, 164
glider training 43–4
GM 125, 133
Gopalan (the Project Director 95–6, 146
Govind, M.K. 121–2
Govindaraj, K. 80

HAL 19–20, 24, 27–30, 34–40, 44, 58, 63–6, 73, 84–6, 88, 90–3, 96, 98–9, 101, 103–5, Design Bureau engineers 30; IJT of

150; Koraput 140; Lucknow 106; Nashik 106, 140; software joint venture 122
Hanamanth, Sudham 64, 66, 96
Handa, Sqn. Ldr. Sudarshan 49–50
Hands on Throttle and Stick (HOTAS) 79
Harinarayana, Kota 38–9, 62, 67, 86, 89, 91, 92, 93, 98, 100, 104, 106, 113, 115, 120, 137; DRDO award for Technology Development 132; Director of Aeronautical Development Establishment (ADE) 19–20, 25, 30, 36; left for Indian Institute of Science 145; Programme Director 125
Hawk AJT 59
Head Up Display (HUD) 75, 191
Helmet Mounted Display (HMD) 163
HF-24 Marut 135
Hindustan Piston Trainer-32 (HPT-32), 57–8
Hindustan Turbo Trainer-34 (HTT-34) 57–8
HT-2 propeller 44
Hulme, Keith 74

In Flight Simulation (IFS) 76–7, 130
Inamdar, Satish 45
Independent Verification and Validation (IV&V) 73
Indian Aircraft Act 1934 121
Indian Airlines Dornier 228; crash in Kochi 119
Indian Space Research Organization (ISRO) 27, 29
indigenization of crucial aircraft sub-systems 100; of decision-making 126
Indo-Pak war 46–7, 139
Inertial Navigation System (INS) 78
Infosys 133
Initial Operational Clearance (IOC) 160, 162
Institute of Aerospace Medicine, Bangalore 129
Intermediate Jet Trainer (IJT) 138,164; and ALH 158; prototype 156
Iron Bird 68, 90–3, 103–4, 105–18, 122, 130, 147, 150; hardware 93; tests 104–5; Request For Action (RFA) 113
Israel Aircraft Industries (IAI) 75

Jaguar strike aircraft 58
Janakiraman, AM 114
Jayavelu, DGAQA inspector 133
Jet Fuel Starter (JFS), 35; Euro II 99; developed by the Engine Design Bureau of HAL, 99
Jet Training Wing Secunderabad, 45
Joint Trials Panning and Evaluation Group (JTPEG) 59
Jung, A.H. 120

Kahai, Flt. Lt 'Kay' Dilmohan Singh 50–3
Kalam, A.P.J. Abdul 34, 62, 65, 84, 86, 91, 93, 98, 104, 159; for Technology Demonstrator (TD) aircrafts 34
Kargil, Pakistan army in 110–11
Karunakar, K. 73
Kaul, ACM 40, 86, 110
Kaveri engine 164
Key Result Areas (KRAs) 68–9
Khan, Field Marshal Ayub 47
Khokhar, Air Cmde. Parvez 150, 156
Khola, H.S. (the Director General of Civil Aviation) 119–20
Kiran 36
Kiran MK I and MK II 57
Kothiyal, Wg. Cdr. Rajiv (Kothi)

19–24, 63, 81, 88–9, 108–9, 101–2, 112, 115, 124–5, 141; nomination for Iven Kinchloe Award 25–6; for Kirti Chakra 131–2; pilot TD-1 117
Krishna, Sqn. Ldr. Suneet, rear seat pilot 128, 142
Krishnaswamy, S. (Kitcha) 37, 78, 144, 149, 157; as AOC-in-C Western Air Command in Delhi 130; as Air Commodore 31; Director Air Staff Requirements 31
Kumar, Dr Srinath 74–5, 88, 93, 132; of the CLAW 120
Kumar, Yogesh (Chairman HAL, GM AR&DC) 106, 125, 132, 158
Kunte, Wg. Cdr 66, 85, 90

Lal, Behari 125
Lamba, AVM A.S. 36
Latif, Air Chief Marshal I.H. 27
Lear jet 80, 89
Light Attack Helicopter (LAH) 153; *see also* Advanced Light Attack Helicopter
Light Combat Aircraft (LCA) 19; and IJT projects 144, 125; TD-1 roll out ceremony 86–7, 91; Technology Demonstrator (TD) 15, 62–3; Team 16; named as Tejas 158; its CLAW 75–7
Limited Series Production (LSP) 145
Line Replaceable Units (LRU) 98
Lockheed Martin (LM) 92, 99–100; 117, 147; Flight Control Division, at Binghampton, New York 146–7
Lou Knotts 80; and Rakesh Sharma 89

Mahajan, Regional Director 125
Mahindra, Raj, MD of the HAL Design Bureau 29–30
Martin Marietta Control Systems (MMCS) of the USA 34, 91–2, 147; digital fly-by-wire technology 32; engineers 73
Marut (HF-24) 28
Marut trainer 60
Mathew, Mrs Mercy 128
McMahon, Air Marshal M. 159–60
Mean Time Between Overhaul (MTBO) 145–6
Messerschmitt, Bolkow & Blohm (MBB) of Germany 29
Microsoft 133
Mig Bison 148
Mig-21 27–8, 162; aircraft of Soviet origin 55; Bis upgrade in 37–8; modified with a Nav/Attack System 59
Mig-23 BN 59
Mig-29 79
Mikoyan Design Bureau Moscow 40
Mirage 2000 21, 79, 82; KT 205 114; trainer 130; its radar on TD-1 124
Mirage III fighter 57
Misra, Cdr. B.B. 75–6, 80, 89, 155
Mohanty, N.R. 64, 140, 144, 157, 159
Mohapatra, Kamini Kantha 64
Multi Function Display (MFDs) 63, 77–8, 106, 111–12
Multi Mode Radar (MMR) 28, 66–8, 93, 149, 160–2, 164–5; indigenous 133
Musharraf, Pervez 36
Mystere 50

Nadkarni, Wg. Cdr. 'Natty' D.R. 60
Nagalia, Air Commodore A.K. 144, 150

Nagraj, K. CE CEMILAC 19, 124
Naidu 'Bob' instructor 43
Nair, Dr C.G.K. (Chairman HAL), 106, 122, 138–9, 159; the Padma Shree 132
Nambiar, Wg. Cdr. Raghunathan 21–3, 82, 87, 101, 111, 117, 124–5, 141–2
Naqvi, DCAS, AM 93
Narain, Yogendra (Defence Secretary) 138
Narayanan, K.G. 78, 91, 102, 122, 128, 132, 139, 148; DRDO award for Technology Development 132
Nashik Design Bureau 36
National Aerospace Laboratories (NAL) 74
National Flight Test Centre (NFTC) 19, 39, 64, 79, 100, 111; pilots 79, 88; team for all flight test activities 127
Nilima 41, 57
nose wheel steering (NWS) system 108–9
NT- 33 82

108 Squadron 110
Operational Flight Programme (OFP) 83
Operational Readiness Platform (ORP) 52
Original Equipment Manufacturer (OEM) 140
Owens, Rich 95, 100

PAF B-57 Pakistan 50
Pai, Dr T.G. 90
Parrag, Mike 80
Patney, AM Vinod 130
Peer, Jeff 89
Performance Verification Committee (PVC) 104
Pilot (initiated) Built In Test (PBIT) 22
Pilot in Loop (PIL) tests 111–13
Pilotless Target Aircraft (PTA) 59
Pokharan nuclear tests 99
Prahalad, Dr T.S. 38–9, 89; as Director, NAL 90
Prasad, Sqn. Ldr. M.K.R. 101–2, 112–13
Prasad, Shailaja 73
Precision Approach Path Indicator (PAPI) 56
pressure error correction (PEC) 93
probability of loss of control (PLOC) 71
Professor Nagabhushna 125, 126
Programme Coordination Team (PCT) 86
Project Definition Phase (PDP); LCA 30
PV-1 and PV-2 102; FRRB 34, 144, 160
PV-2 134, Tejas prototype vehicle 162

R-13F jet engine for the Mig-21 59
R-60 CCM missile firing trials 58
Rai, Air Marshal J.S. 21; AOC-in-C Training Command 125, 129
Rajkumar, Philip as Air Commodore 61; awarded a Mention-in-Despatches 55; awarded Param Vishisht Seva Medal (PVSM) 113; awarded the Ati Vishisht Seva Medal (AVSM) 61; awarded Vayu Sena Medal (VM) 61; became a Group Captain 61; Chief Test Pilot (CTP) 57; course at Defence Services Staff College (DSSC) 60; deputed to Iraqi Air Force 61; Director of ADA 158; enrolled in NCC Air Wing 43;

Fighter Combat Leader's course 60; Instrument Rating Examiner 60; member of Air Marshal C.V. Gole Committee, 58; posted as Director, Air Staff Requirements (DASR) 37; posted to Aircraft and Systems Testing Establishment (ASTE) 57; posted to No. 1 'Tiger' Squadron 46; promoted to Flight Lieutenant 55; promoted to Wg. Cdr. 60; promoting to AOC-in-C's grade 139; retired 160; selected for Air Force Flying College (AFFC) 44; set-up the NFTC 161; suggested the number as KH-2001 123; training at French Test Pilots School at Istres 56–7; visit to Warton 83-4; visited Israel 74–5; with ACM 103–4
Raju, K.N. 84
Ramage, Jim 89
Ramalingam 78
Ramchand, K. 67
Ramsheshan, Dr of CEMILAC 91
Rao, K.P. (Head of Structures, Department of Aerospace Engineering) 125
Rao, K.V.L. 96, 98–9, 120, 125, 145
Rao, P.N.A.P. Project Director Avionics 112
Rao, P.V. Narasimha 34, 86
Rao, Sriramachandra 122
Raveendran, Wg. Cdr. P.K. (Ravi) 21–3, 64, 85, 99, 101, 113, 152
Ray, Vice Admiral S.K. 11, 91, 104
Reagan, Ronald 31
Real Time Simulator (RTS) 76, 77, 105, 120, 130, 133; in FORTRAN 92
Reddy, Subba of HAL AR&DC 106, 132; as Iron Bird team 91
rescue procedures 129
RFA proforma 136
Rohini 28
Rosoboronexport officials in Moscow 149
Royal College of Defence Studies in London, UK 36

Sahni, Air Cmde R.D. 60
Sarabhai Space Centre 125
Sareen, ACM S.K. 87, 103, 107; as Air Marshal 90
Sargodha raid 51–5
Sathyaraja of ADE 111
Satur, Sqn. Ldr. Denny 'Denzil' 46, 49–50
Search and Rescue (SAR) duties 129
secondary power system (SPS) 96
Sekhon, Air Marshal (AOC-in-C) M.S. 116
Self-Protection Jammer (SPJ) Electronic Warfare (EW) 58
Shankar, Sqn. Ldr. Uday 63, 80, 82, 89; Flight Test Engineer (FTE) 63–4; premature retirement 101
Shanks, Gerry 92
Sharma, Wg. Cdr. Rakesh (India's first Cosmonaut) 63, 88–9, 98, 101; Cdr CTP, HAL 125
Sharma, Ram Niwas (Chairman, HAL) 39, 86, 106
Singh, Sqn. Ldr. Baldev 63, 80, 88–9, 101, 156
Singh, Air Marshal K.B. 90
Singh, V.P. 32
Singh, Wg. Cdr. Vikram (test pilot) 150, 159
Singh, B.D. 145
Smith, Terry 85, 104, 117
Society of Experimental Test Pilots (SETP) USA 25; recognition of 60
Sreevatsan General Manager (AR&DC) 84

Structural Coupling Test (SCT) 107
Sukhi, Sqn. Ldr. 64, 90
Sukhoi 22 swing-wing fighter 59
Sukumar, Gp. Capt. 138
Suresh, B.N. 125–6
Swedish Gripen programme 136, 139

T-33 89
T-6G Texan 44
Tactics and Combat Development Establishment (TACDE) 56, 60
Tactics and Combat, Training and Development Squadron (T&C, D&TS) 56
Taneja, Om Prakash 'Omi' (Wing Commander) 46, 48–51, 55
taxi test 105–18
Technology Demonstrator-1 (TD-1) 19, 35, 63, 100, 108, 113, 119, 120, 128, 134, 157; last round of tests 123
Technology Demonstrator-2 (TD-2) 101; was readied for its first EGR 134, 141, 143, 157
Teng, Li 146
Test Pilots School (TPS) at ASTE 60, 64, 150
Tipnis, Air Chief Marshal Anil 19, 103, 107–8, 114, 120, 122, 125, 130
'Top Gun' school 56
trainer, Mig-21 69, 138
Transport Training Wing, Begumpet 45
Turbine Inlet Temperature (TIT) 146

United States Air Force (USAF) 45, 76; helps Indian DRDO 31
Upadhya, A.R. 108
US Navy fighter F-14 135
USA, technology transfer sanctions imposed by 15, 30–1, 46, 95–105, 120, 126, 130, 141, 147–8, 161

Vajpayee, Atal Behari 139, 156
Valluri, S.R. (Director-General of ADA) 29–30
Verma, M.B. 'Frisky' 47, 145, 160
Vishweshwariya, Wg. Cdr. 78
VISTA (Variable in Flight Simulation Trainer Aircraft) 88
Vohra, Gautamski 64

Weller, BAe consultant 112
Widger, Harry 74
Wipro 133
Wisner, Frank 86
Wright Laboratories of the USAF 16, 72, 76, 77, 113

Yadav, Sharad 119, 121

Zakak, Nagui 95–6, 146